LAST CALL

New Poems

DAVID LEE

San Antonio, Texas
2014

Last Call © 2014
by David Lee

Cover: Judge Roy Bean's Jersey Lilly Bar. Photograph by Jan Lee.
Author photography by Jan Lee and Shae Van Wagoner.

ISBN: 978-1-60940-375-1 (paperback original)

E-books:

ePub: 978-1-60940-376-8
Mobipocket/Kindle: 978-1-60940-377-5
Library PDF: 978-1-60940-378-2

Wings Press
627 E. Guenther
San Antonio, Texas 78210
Phone/fax: (210) 271-7805
On-line catalogue and ordering:
www.wingspress.com

Wings Press books are distributed to the trade by
Independent Publishers Group
www.ipgbook.com

Cataloging In Publication:

Lee, David, 1944 August 13-
  [Poems. Selections]
  Last call : new poems / David Lee.
      pages cm
  "Wings Press books are distributed to the trade by Independent Publishers
Group"--T.p. verso.
  Includes bibliographical references.
  ISBN 978-1-60940-375-1 (pbk. : alk. paper) -- ISBN 978-1-60940-376-8
(ePub ebook) -- ISBN 978-1-60940-377-5 (Mobipocket ebook) -- ISBN 978-
1-60940-378-2 (pdf)
  I. Title.
  PS3562.E338A6 2014
  811'.54--dc23
                              2013043117

Contents

For Eloise and Jan

who kept us for the most part on the high road

LAST CALL

Our revels now are ended.

—Prospero
The Tempest, IV, i

Reveille, Adolph's

Lake Hills, Texas

Rena working the bar past John Sims
with the coffee pot asked

Yall boys going
to the School Board Meeting tonight?

Clovis said I don't imagine I will
but Billy has to go
since he's nominated
to be on a hoity toity committee

Billy said
I doubt I'll be there either

Rena said What committee
and what's hoity toity?

Billy said Part A is meaningless
and as for Part B
according to the Oxford English Dictionary
hoity toity in the denotative sense
comes directly down to la dee fucking dah

It says that in the dictionary?

Clovis said If Billy said it is
it's exactly verbatim
which to him means
that's the gist of it

Billy said Ledbitter
you don't know Jack Shit

That shows what you know
I might have known him once

Oh bull said Billy
you rattle on as much
as that damned old Dodge pickup of yours
you old high pockets

Rena said Now you boys
yall just straighten up and act respectable
this is a high class joint
and it's too early for yall arguing
when real people mostly can't even understand
what you two ex-professors are saying

Clovis said As a matter of fact
I remember it all now and I believe I did
I think he might have lived
in Tahoka a while back
and I could have met him there

Yeah and in what part of a Chaucerian pig's anatomy
do you think we'll believe that? said Billy

Would yall like a bump on your coffee?

Naw we better get going
make hay while the sun's shining said Billy

Rats to kill said Clovis

What yall got planned? said Rena

Dunno yet said Clovis
haven't had time to think about it so far

Got to see what the weather's going to do said Billy

Looks to be a purdy one

Well I hope so said Billy

If it gets hot we can sit on the porch
and shade bake, tell some lies

Might haul some garbage

Mebbe go down and count Delphin's three cows said Clovis
You can write about it again
now that you know for sure how many there are

Billy said See what I mean?
Ledbitter, you never did know Jack Shit

That's right
I probably wouldn't recognize him
if I was sitting right beside him
would I?

I bet yall find something interesting
at least to talk about said Rena

Let's go Klogphorne
we're burning up sunshine

Yep said Billy up and at'm

Bye yall

Yes'm

Bye Miss Rena

See yall tomorrow morning

Bright and early said Billy
unless we decide to hold the School Board Meeting here tonight
then we'll be back with the libationous expeditionary force

I imagine that's a fact said Rena
I'll be looking for you either way
either time
you boys be good now

Yes'm Miss Rena
unless we get lucky

Will you come on Clovis my godamitey
I've been standing here half the morning
waiting on you already

You just button it up Buffalo Billy Bob Klepfrog
I told you I'm coming
save your breath to cool your mush
Mr In a Big Hurry

Well you're sure not

Bye, see you later, said John
See yall tonight I'm betting

From what I've heard
you pretty much only bet on sure things
so we'll probably be here

I spect that's right said John
I'll be here awaiting

The Traildust Gospel

¡Contempla!
—Juan Bautista, who, folk legend tells us,
lost his mind over a woman's footprints
in the dust somewhere east of Pecos

1

Onella Penny smoked a pipe
P. A. tobacco you could smell
two yards over
nobody ever mentioned
outside our neighborhood
but what finally made her famous
after the big stomp
was when we noticed
how she walked so hard
for a woman who wasn't
to speak of necessarily
fleshy

      in a dry season
her steps wove dust
cyclone children on the way
to the trash barrel or clothes line
past her ankles, swirls
almost to her knees
so that

      one August morning
Billy Klogphorne and Clovis Ledbitter
perched on the back porch furniture
morning coffeeing in short sleeved shirts
saw her emerge like Venus

in an ocean of heat waves
with a kitchen trash
bucket

        footstep whirlwinds
all around her back yard, in immaculate Texanese
Clovis said One them air dust devils
gets under her housecoat
up her nightgown arising
she'll lift herself
like a full grown female angel
right off the ground
I bet

        she
looked smartly their way
so Billy couldn't laugh or take the wager
leaned over and pretended
something in his coffeecup
needed to be looked at
anything else right then
was not going to be worth the chance

2

Then the day Marvin Penny
came outside
looking like second place
in a two entrant
world champion fist whipping
she became
legend

        neither one surprised
after they heard the scream

through the housewalls across the yard
to the back porch PBR libations
when she learned the rumor
of his gallavantation with Kim Pierce
Billy in perfect Tejano splendor said

                                          Clovis

that isn't no knucklebumps on his head
you get up and look close
I'll put two dollars
yougn see a clear footprint
from his busted lip
up between and past
that eye'll be swolt black tomorrow
with a bloody nose in the middle
Clovis said No bet
that looks to be a fact

3

When Cephas Bilberry heard
at the Dew Drop Inn that night
he said Well I hope Marvin he learnt
a lesson from it either way
whatever it was needing
such immediate education
Billy said I imagine he did
Cephas said That being what?
Billy said Next time
he gets knocked on his ass
he'll make sure he falls face down
so the following foot marks
don't show

                    Cephas
said You mean
whoever did that stomp
it was after he'd already been knocked down?
Clovis said
Unless she can walk around in the air
stomping on heads, you know
a better way?

                    Billy said
If it's a point
needs to be made
or a trailway to be commended
it might as well be stated proper
so the muckling effort
doesn't need to be repeated

                         Cephas
said Well that might be right
Clovis said Yep
ever footstep in this drought
raises a genuine cyclome or leaves a print
sometimes permanent
and that's not blowing smoke
or preacher talk
and Cephas said Godamitey's mama
aint it the truth?

          4

Juan Diego Mendietta
unloading a case of Pabst's Blue Ribbon beer
into the ice cooler at the Dew Drop Inn
heard a voice
saying A woman who walked in air

left a footprint on the face
of Marvin Penny
that could be seen clearly
with one's own eyes

                that night
he told Father Gutierrez
the things he heard but the Padre
shook his head sadly and said No my son
these are the words of a fool
drunk on bootleg beer
you must try to remember
milagros almost never occur in Tejas
where there are too many gringos
for the Lord's work

              so
Juan Diego Mendietta
went home in despair
his hope of imparting a miracle's appearance
shattered like his youthful dreams
of making love to Hooter Hagins
but he told his wife Eva who some said
was de la familia de las brujas
while he ate the tacos she made for him
what he heard spoken clearly
who told

         her sister Maria Calvones
who told her cousin Isabel Ramones
who cleaned Onella Penny's house
every Monday from nine en la manana
until la hora de cuatro in the afternoon
who went to the Penny casa
the next morning even though it was a Thursday
and knocked

when he
opened his door he said
You aint posta be here today yet
it aint Monday is it?
she screamed and pressed her hands to her cheeks
the indelible print of a foot
clearly visible on Marvin Penny's face
!Madre de dios! she screamed
he said What the hell?
but Isabel Ramones turned and ran
down the calle shouting
!Es un Milagro! !Un Milagro!

soon
votary candles appeared nightly on the porch
of Onella and Marvin Penny's home
which he removed and threw
into the garbage barrel in his dusty back yard
until Onella stopped him saying
You leave those goddam things
right where they are and he said
Yes dear

entonces
for a decade the casa de Penny
became a flickering shrine to the miraculous
footprint of the Virgin seen by many
including Juan Diego Mendietta
who was said to be the first witness
and Isabel Ramones who gave the miracle
confirmation

and it came to pass
at last Onella died of consumption
and el viejo Marvin Penny grew old and sacred
the hairs of his head white as snow

and en la tarde when he went
into his dusty yard
to sit in the warm sun and remember
all those events of his life
that never actually occurred
la gente would come to his house
to sit at his knees and view his face
where at times

          when the light
shone from the exact right angle
a small perfect footprint
could been seen by a select few
who were chosen to be witness
and the paisanos would touch his shoulders
and the denim fabric of his clothing
whispering to him
beseeching forgiveness

The Monument to the South Plains

Son
your mama who is admittedly a hair trigger weeper
walked all the way down to the barn to tell me
she is genuinely and purely exasperated to tears
with your sitting in here on your bed alone
for three days now wrapped up in divine and superfluous
thought over God knows what and that I
should unleash and afflict upon you a stampede
of accumulated wisdom in order to provide incentive
and momentum for possible confession and redemption
or in other words what in the world is the matter?
your mama really wants to know the cause of your pesteration

Willy John said Nothing's wrong Daddy
I have to make a project in indigenous sculpture
for my Physical Art thesis and I'm trying
to come up with a mental design and materials
with not a lot of luck so far that I can speak of

Behold a wonder said a poet
you were named for once beneath a time Son
out behind the very barn where I have been piddling
all morning rests a considerable bevy of red bricks and paving stones
off to the starboard side used cinder blocks and dead concrete forms
on the larboard side a minor subaltern deity's ransom
of worn out farm equipment my daddy put out for years
wondering if there would ever be any use for it
before the Second Coming or the Russian bomb
inside the barn seven sacks of ready-mix concrete
along with arc and acetylene welders and even a soldering iron
I would be just as happy as a crow
that found a dropped plate of communion wafers

if you could utilize that indigenous scrap material
so that it would seem I had a purpose all along
for my years of unrequited salvage, separation and stacking

You got any ideas about what it could be?

Nosir
you go out there and stare at it for a while
if you need lessons on that talent I'm available for instruction
I'll bring along a chair if it takes too long
drawing up a mental plan of opportunity
to endure and prevail as the other man
you were named after once said
build your sculpture any way you want it
as long as it looks good from the kitchen window to your mama
as a monument for the rest of her life
to your teenage years and when you are done
we will call it the Statue of Limitations
until a better title comes along
anytime during construction you think it's gone wrong
give the word I'll knock it down with the tractor
you can start again until you get it right

Willy John built three, tore down the first two
finally settling on a tower amalgamated between an obelisk
and a Babel ziggurat, a spiral of plough shares
fenders and motor covers, tractor seats and steering wheels
a corn planter, spring tooth harrow and flat cultivator
manure spreader, deep trench, disc cultivator and windrower
all manner of painted and rusting equipment
conjoined invisible in the warp and woof, the new body
arose from a blood red brick base
and a gathering of barbed wire strung against
an open side like it emerged from the skeleton
of an overlooked and dying chthonic deity
an androgynous Texas god resurrected and ascending from the barnyard

straining against gravity's death clutch
and his father's terrible acrophobia
grasping upward into nothing more than still air
building materials so heavy and bundlesome that at last
Willy John devised and constructed a fifty eight foot derrick
with a block and tackle pulley system to hoick up
a John Deere engine block a magically and technically impossible
six feet above the rig: a great skull atop the megalith
a pair of steel irrigation pipes protruding
like massive horns upward from the sides

after the last arc weld lightning burst
the final acetylene flame, the penultimate binding smear
of cement, wrap of bailing wire, spit and glue
he brought his parents to stand beside the barn
and view the Monument to the South Plains
rising from the abandoned feed lot
and his father trembled, his mother wept
as if she were viewing the birth of a new grand child
before the great sculpture soughing with the wind's movement
marking the pathway trace of light's footfall
on the near horizon a ripening field of cotton
and behind, knee deep in the white foam of crop
three scattered pump jacks, their rise and fall
like the distant shapes of migrant pickers
working their slow way through the half mirage
My Lord, he said, Willy John, that thing's alive

E. U. Washburn's Story:
Uncle Abe

I have not wasted my life
—Richard Shelton, "Desert Water"

Genesis 17:7

1

Oncet when I was a boy
a walking man come
to town twicet every year
folks didn't know who he was
name him Uncle Abe
said he was lost and wandering
in his own mind
a harmless old thing just passing by

carried this paper bag in his hand
no child nor cat can not find out what's in
I sidled him in the gravel road said
Mister Man, what you got in that paper sack?

he turnt round looked me up and down
like a rooster hypnotized
by a line in the sand
said Master Boy, I'll tell you what I brought
but you answer me first one thing
you say how many years your mama's got
I told and he said Not enough
tell me your grandmama's home
I said she aint she's dead and gone

2

he said
I was a almost whole live grown up boy oncet
like you walking along soon
had me a paper sack of store bought candy
going down the road
after work at the cotton gin
girlchild womern on her poach call me say
Mister Man, what you got in that possible sack?
come here show me right now
patted beside her where for me to set
I come to her she say What you bring?
I shook all over
she was beautiful as churchhouse sin
I felt as ugly as the real thing

she eat a piece without asking
I known deep in my paper sack it was
one chocolate covenant hiding to be last
pretty soon we almost racing
eating that candy so fast
she lay one smiling piece on her tongue
with her finger say Come here
put her mouth on mine
she pass me that seed
take it back and again
till the covenant was gone
then so was she
all but the memory

I had me one wife, son
four good chirren grown up
left and gone
but never nothing
like that day since come along

now I got *hope* and *mebbe*
and then whatall time's left
this paperbag of sweet candy
with one covenant
for her somewhere waiting
if I'm so blessed

3

he told me his story that day
again every time since twicet a year
till the day he didn't come here
I never stopped remembering
the promise I made
to never have to say
I got no more of my life to waste
I still try to look
down every street
at every porch
every old walking man's face
every shadowed place

4

oncet mama say
Don't you be shiftless boy
don't you daydream your life away
pretty soon you be walking lonesome
empty head and pocket
like that crazy Uncle Aberham
kicking rocks down the gravel road

I said Oh Mama Mama
don't even promise that might be so
it's a whole live world
inside that lucky man
you and all the rest of this town
don't even know
one sweet covenant
you caint never understand

Kay Stokes' First Visitation

I'll buy that sculpture from you

It's not for sale
but you deem it a sculpture

Everything's for sale and yes I do

Not everything

Yougn about name your price

I won't sell it but I also
can't sell it, it's not mine

Whose is it?

My son made it
I suppose he owns it
or my wife
or even my daddy the original provider
maybe we all do
or maybe none of us
maybe it owns itself
What would you do with it?

I'd move it over to my place

If you could get it there
It wouldn't fit
it was made to be right here

Maybe I could make it fit
Ign hire a way to get it there

Maybe you couldn't make it fit
then it would be neither useful nor ornamental
about like an erection on a mule

They say you got a way with words

They

Yep

The great arbiter of all knowledge
opinion and attitude in the known world
extending to the Texas borders

Pretty much
some say furthern that
You caint tell me you couldn't use the money
even if you are a retired perfessor and all

No I can't tell you that

But you won't sell it

Why do you want it so much?
when you first noticed it you were quoted as saying
it was the ugliest thing you'd ever seen

Changed my mind

Why? Isn't that a rarity?

Cause there aint another one around
I'd like for it to belong to me
I'd just like to say it was mine

Like about everything else in Garza County

Pretty much

Overheard Conversation
Between Billy Klogphorne
and his son William, age 16,
a Few Years Back

Being your own man
is a good thing, Willy
it's a first step
towards economic
independence

which is an oxymoron
and self-reliance
which may be a status
more attainable
at this juncture

but you need to understand
being your own self-reliant man
means one thing:
making a map ahead of time
to find your way out of Hell

which is damned close
to the sum total
of everything on earth I've learned
up to this particular juncture
                    in the process

At the Sign of the Flying Red Horse

1

Monroe Newberry
coming down the street pushing his bicycle
front tire flopping like a wet flag
into Johnny Bert Ezell's filling station
What you got there, Monroe? he said

Monroe pointed at his bicycle, then at the tire, nodded

I can see that
it's a green one that uster be a Western Flyer
by its looks
before it got to be a personal modified
version of something else
you want to use the bay
yougn go back and patch that tire

Monroe shook his head

You don't know how to fix a flat tire?

Monroe shook his head

Your daddy he never shown you how to?

again

Well
Come on back then
it aint too busy this morning
I'll give you a lesson in how to do it
brang that back here

Okay lay it on its side and turn it upside down
standing up so wegn get to the wheel
now you take a pair of pliars and a monkeyranch
you just uncrack that nut like this
loosen it up to where the wheel comes off
you don't have to take the nut all the way off

it's a little harder on a back tire
you'll have to work it around the chain
you just aloosen it right here and slip it off the cog wheel
then it'll be pretty much the same thing with it, too

Okay you take and bring the wheel
over here on the bench and get you a flat head screwdriver
put it right here under the tire edge
prize it up like this over the rim
so now work that screwdriver down
lifting the whole tire edge over the rim, see?
if it's giving resistance and closing back up behind as you go
take and put the pliars handle up here
holt it open and now work that tire
all the way around until it's off the rim all over

Okay
you reach in underneath
get this inner tube out from under the tire
being careful not to jerk out the valve stem
push it through its hole like this
and take that inner tube off the wheel

bring it over to the air hose and fill it up
now put it in a bucket of water or run a waterhose over it like this
you'll see and mebbe hear the air hole
right there you see it? mark it with your finger
bring it back over to the bench and get your tire patching kit

I suppose you don't have one here's what it looks like
you can get you one at Bill Edwards Hardware and Appliance
it'll last you almost a lifetime

take this lid off the can you see the rough edge part on it?
scrape that air hole with it like this
rough it up so the suption will hold
now get out the glue, see?
squirt a little over that roughed part and the hole
spread it out and blown on it a little

next shake the rubber patches out of the can
find you one that will cover the hole
yours is a little one so I'd use a small patch
if they all gone cut a big one down to size
now pull off the hesive cover on the back of the patch
so the sticky side's out
just put that sonofagun right over that air hole
press down and smoothen it out
to where it's neatened and flat, you see?

before you put it back in the tire eyeball measure
from the valve stem to the patch where the hole was
take and run your finger on the inside of the tire to where that is
so yougn find out what made the flat tire
there it is, see? that's a goathead you runned over
so turn the tire over on the outside of where your finger is
see, it's right there
you'll need to get that sticker out with your fingers
or some pliars if you can't get purchase on it

it'd pay you in the long run to sweep your fingers all down
the inside of your tire to see if it's any other stickers poking through
yougn bust off the sharpies mebbe pick the stems out from the tread
save yourself doing it all over again before too long
if yougn get your daddy to give you a quarter

go down to Bill Edwards and buy you a tube of neverleak
and put it in, that'll stop most goathead flats

now we put that inner tube back
on the wheel getting the valve stem in straight
work that tire back around the rim over the inner tube like this
take your screwdriver and put it under the tire
lift it up and see, it just pops back on
so we'll air it up to 30
now we put this wheel back on the forks
tighten the nut up with the monkeyranch
and there you go. Done.
You think you can do it now?

Do what? said Monroe Newberry

Well I'll swan said Johnny Bert Ezell
I thought you might speak one day
and here it is

                                        2

Did you hear a word I said, boy?
I was ashowing you how to do it and telling you
all the way
Didn't you hear?

Monroe nodded

But you can't do it yourself now
after watching me and telling you what to do?

Monroe scrunched his shoulders

Well then, that'll be a quarter, son

What for? said Monroe

That's good said Johnny Bert Ezell
For fixing your flat tire
it costes a quarter

Monroe held out his empty hands

What you got then?

Monroe shook his head
then put his hand in his pocket
pulled out a pocket knife

Give it here

Monroe shook his head

Why not? said Johnny Bert Ezell

shook his head again

Tell me said Johnny Bert Ezell

Daddy's said Monroe

Hegn get it back
I'll have it right here
hegn come for it
Johnny Bert Ezell held out his hand

Monroe scrunched his shoulders again

It'll be all right said Johnny Bert Ezell
I'm not gone keep it

Monroe put the knife in his hand
then pointed to the bicycle

Yep, she's ready to go

Monroe swung his leg over the bike
looked at Johnny Bert Ezell and said
See you

I'll hope it'll be sooner than later
said Johnny Bert Ezell

                                                    3

You took my pocketknife
away from my boy Monroe
said D'Wayne Newberry

That's not ezactly right said Johnny Bert Ezell
he owed me a quarter and he didn't have one
he give me that knife as collateral

What'd he own you a quarter for?
said D'Wayne Newberry

Fixing a flat tire

You charge a quarter for that?
it uster be a dime

Inflation said Johnny Bert Ezell
like the livestock man says on the radio
higher higher higher that's the way it goes

That wadn't his pocketknife
it's mine
he didn't have no right to give it to you

Yougn have it back
said Johnny Bert Ezell

I can?

Yessir

Give it here then

Nope, you've got to redeem it

A quarter?

No, I'll need a bit more seeing as it's purloined
it has sentimental value to me now

How much?

About a dollar's worth

A dollar said D'Wayne Newberry
that's almost as much as it costed new

Oh I imagine it cost moren that
Billy Klogphorne he collects pocketknives
I'll bet you he would give me upward
of a dollar for it used

You'd sell my pocketknife to Billy Klogphorne?
I don't have upwards of a dollar on me

Then it's a bargain for you said Johnny Bert Ezell
a dollar and six bits new at least
yougn have this one for a dollar even
and I sharpened the blades

You did?

Yougn shave the hair off your arm with it now
give you something to do at church during the sermon

How'd you know that? said D'Wayne Newberry

I'm not blind I seen you trying
now yougn get it accomplished
impress your girlfriend and boys

I haven't got no dollar on me

How much you got?

I don't know
let me see
quarter thirty five forty fifty five fifty seven cents

Tell you what
just today I'll give you a special deal
I'll redeem this here sharpened pocket knife to you
for fifty seven cents and to ease my conscience over the usury
I'll put that money in the collection plate this Sunday
as long as you'll make me a promise

What?

You'll buy your boy Monroe a patch kit
and teach him how to fix his own flat tire
from now on and if he doesn't learn it
next time it'll be a dollar fifty so that makes it a even better deal
you'll be saving yourself a whole dollar and four bits then
you think you can do that?

I dunno
maybe
he don't learn things too quick

Well, neither do you
but I hope so anyways now give me fifty seven cents
and yougn have this two dollar sharpened knife
we'll call it even

I suppose
somehow this don't seem right
I think you're taking a vantage of me
I'll have to thank about it but I might need that pocketknife
I guessed I don't have no choice

Nope, not today but you do for next time

I do?

Yep
you teach that boy how to take care of his equipment
it's gone save you a whole lot of money
time and trouble in the long run
I guarantee you that for a fact
so in that light you actually got a real bargain
you can be proud of negotiating

I hope the rest of your day goes real good for you
and that sharpened pocket knife makes you a good one
and for that boy of yours Monroe who incidentally
needs to be coming to my Sunday School class
at ten o'clock sharp this weekend
I hope you catch my drift

Bye now
say hey to that boy Monroe

San Antonio Incident

Jerry Ray Newman on family vacation
ran half a block down the street
to the closest public pay phone
when the Operator said Number please
he said Can yall send a amblance
down here real quick
my mama she's hurt purdy good?

Can you tell me how she's hurt?

Walking down the street
here come this big goddam sowbitch
jalapeno pig with babies
her being a fleshy woman
she couldn't run as fast as the rest of us
it caught her and mault her real bad
she's a bleeding like a sieve
on that one leg

What is the location?

Right down the street from the motel
where we're staying at

Can you give me an address?

What's the address, Daddy?
he says it's 4th street and Rhododendron

Could you please spell that?

Wait. Hey Daddy
Okay, we'll carry her piggyback
up a block to 4th street and Fir
that's F, I, R
she's a hollering in a embarrassing manner
Daddy said could you ask that amblance
to get here in a hurry?

Driving Solo: Clovis Rants
A Monologue in Five Acts with Intermission

I am but mad north-northwest:
when the wind is southerly
I know a hawk from a handsaw
—Shakespeare, *Hamlet*

1

Good windy day morning ladies and all you
notsowannabe gentlemen buckaroos
for the Pulitzer-level literati
it's going to be a Captain Call's half-broke wild mare romp
a genuine frost breath horrible tempered mean rodeo bucker
you'd rather milk than ride day
swirling winds out of the south 30 to 35 upwards
gusts running right up to the 60's, cloudy with highs in the low 40's
dropping
you stay inside right here with KJZZ
we'll play you some windy day jazz tunes
stay saddled up right here to get you through the soaring sand dunes
we'll buck you right to the moon
the man in his own words said at six o'clock this very morning
and I'm driving alone without Jan down the slurry seal into Jack-
pot, Nevada
listening to jazz, the morning sage and Raft River bank brush
bent frostquivering willowwhite
and the road kill breakfast club buzzards
flap flapping across my window like sleetwind
sky curdled into thunderbumpers
gas tank three quarters leaning on half
Miles slouched over my tiny mind
blowing Bye bye Blackbird

because I'm driving all alone
five hundred and thirty-seven more miles
to where I'll sleep tonight
and thirteen hundred more before I hit
the Hill Country in three days running
down the road listening to my new storeboughten Jackpot
Greatest All Time Jazz cassette
out of the dollar sale bin at Cactus Pete's gift shop

Jan behind me in Twin Falls, Idaho nursing
her bellyache mother through another season's
episode of whatever she's dreamed up
to be going around this time
me heading across the sagebrush backside
of Nevada about a hundred and three miles
from godforgotten Ely down to a half tank
into yessir Mr. D. J., an exactly HellBitch headwind
blowing slantwise out of Nogales, Mexico
elegant Duke giving over to raucous Dizzy
shifting down to *Blue Train* granny gear in a fifty mile stretch
rattling my pickup like a snaredrum
pushing the beat across Coltrane's
and my, too, fried brain

driving through the desert hurricane
down the road straight south
listening to jazz by myself
approaching the intersection of the designated
Loneliest Highway in America

gas tank now down to one third
twelve miles per gallon dropping by the lurch
looking square across to the quarter line
range cows with washboard ribs
standing butt to the nettlewind bawling
like the last bellhounds at the end of time
Dizzy reappearing to tell me
we all play the same notes
the way I get from one note to the next
that's my style
and there's not a single thing I can do
out here in the wasteland but nod
and hold the truck on the road
in my tightfisted style
right up to the red insanity mark line
I can't break concentration
to argue with my man
acknowledging pissed off as I am
with the circumstances
what I'm giving is all I've got

Interlude
at McDonalds in Ely, Nevada, drinking coffee
after filling up my truck with stagecoach-robbery
priced diesel
ten point two m.p.g.

shadebaked wind children outside the fast-food walls
finger and nose prints pressed into windowpeeped glass
tiny hands beating against the invisible boundary
between light and light demand entrance
                                        suddenly
eruption of a camperpickupload of tarheel cotton sack ragamuffin
tumbleweeds interrupted from their long southwind roll
to the Oregon border where they might chance align
against a snowdrift fence awaiting castcall
for the Hell's Canyon remake of Deliverance
pour into McDonalds, roiling and clamormongering
this one okay, mama? if it's white people serving I'll eat here
elbow their way forward shouting immediate service demands
what you wanting, mama? you shut up, Billy Don
I aint done reading the dollar menu yet

                                humming
a Bill Evans riff I accept my refill from the young
Ronalda apprentice and while turning to the door
whisper as loudly as humanly possible *best deal in town*
four cream senior coffee half price

                        mama's scream
where does it say that? Billy Don go get him
make him come back and show me whar it's at
I move into sharpwind toward my truck to begin again
driving the road alone listening to jazz

Billy Don

screaming to the glass pane *wait come back heah*
my mama wants you too late, cracker-buddy

I'm on my way

out of Ely with love and squalor
walking along minding my own business with my hot
cuppacoffee on the one way path to my pickup, me
I'm getting myself ready to start the last half of this trip
over with once and for sonofabitching all

4

driving down the road listening to jazz
wishing my wife would once and for all
absolutely, ultimately and irrevocably
finally tell her mama she's got a life of her own
fists of wind beating all about
the head and shoulders of my beat up Dodge truck
knocking it across the road like a spent heavyweight pug
and now Humbolt Pass with a foot of new snow
my thermostat shot to Gehenna or Sheol or Dis or dat and back
heater blowing air as cold as a Newfoundlander's
proverbial shithouse in its archetypal Hades or Acheron
like I know my damned room will be
when I get there in about five and a half hours
alone with Billy Holiday singing me
her personal inspired version of
It aint no love in this town you heading to tonight
driving straight south to hell
or Pioche, whichever comes first

5

on the road listening to jazz
the sun falling like winter sky
horizon imploding into a thousand square miles
of juniper and beercans and roadkill
turning left and heading east at Panaca
I say out loud *thank you Lord that's done and over with*
this last hundred has to be the easy stretch
we've both been waiting on
but the wind the goddammed wind
that never blows out of the east
I'd promised myself
not once in the history of civilized mankind
I'd heard of in this part of the world twists
shouts and rattles its way ninety degrees larboard
laughs and shrieks like a banshee windowpeeking
at a senior rehabilitation center viva voce
everything out here screaming awful
how loud and alone just dammed alone the whole world is
and I have a frosty ninety four
windstarved miles to go before I sleep
Charlie Parker telling me personally
what I need is some good *windy day lonesome blues*
what else on earth do I have left to lose
driving myself down the end of the world road
home to Texas without Jan, listening to jazz

The First Miracle

came to pass when Eva Saenz Mendietta the Seer
some called la Bruja visited the monument
with her family and closely inspected
Willy John's sculpture until her vision
rested upon a spot just above the juncture
Willy John's father designated the half way mark
she closed her eyes for almost three minutes
when she opened them pointed at the indentation and said
Veo la cara de la Virgen and all were sore amazed

Willy John's dad who had known Eva Saenz
for almost fifty years even before
she became Mendietta moved to her side
followed her point to the mark and saw
what could be taken as the image of a face
in the rusted metal and proclaimed Well
Eva turned and whispered You see?
and he said Si, comprendo lo que dices
Muy bien she said and then told her family
It is time for us to go, vamanos muchachos
Willy John's father said Eva, mi amor, you know
you're welcome to come back any time you want
she said softly, Cuidado, novio, if this gets out
it will no longer be a sculpture or monument
it will become a shrine ?listo para eso?
Ready as I'll ever be this time he said
I will come back she said, Yes

Aftermath Evaluation from a Pickup Window

If that's posta be art
I'd like to know what the hell is it

It looks exactly like the ghost
of a burnt out drilling rig said John Sims

Why you think that?

I been in a oil well fire
that's something I know something about
That and ghosts

First Miracle Redux

and the paisanos came to venerate
by the pickup truckloads
many bringing picnic baskets
to stay the afternoon until Willy John's father
had to build and plumb toilet facilities
put out fifty five gallon oil drums for garbage

then the word spread to the gringos
who came in station wagons in order to make damn sure
none of them could ever see a face anywhere
in that stack of piled up scrapjunk
in spite of their best well-intended efforts
many did see the visage after Willy John's father
pointed it out and after he told them
how it could be seen in noonlight and moonlight
how it changed with the changing of the light
he had to put a gate on the road into his property
to keep teenagers out on full moon nights

and then the day when Reverend Coy Stribling
of the Church of God of Prophesy of Holy and Divine Revelation
came to bear witness and tried to follow
the pointline but seemed to be looking
about six feet above said I seen it
I believe that could be the face of Jesus Christ hisself
which was revealed unto me when I was fourteen
when a woman said Reverend Coy
It's posta be a face of the Virgin is what they say it is
he said It aint no virgins except in the Bible
but they been gone from the world a long time ago

when he offered to hold a church service
there on Sunday next For a official dedication

Willy John's daddy said Nope Sorry
we'll keep it secular this time around
and Reverend Coy waxed sore amazed at the turn down

three days later Eva Saenz Mendietta called
to tell Willy John's father
how sorry she was that happened
sometimes she wished she really were a witch
she'd cast a spell to make Coy go away permanently
or maybe one to give him an actual mind
in the place his brain was supposed to be
Willy John's daddy told her he sometimes thought
Jesus got it wrong in the Beatitudes when he said
The meek shall inherit the earth
when all too often it was like the boilings
when they used to make lye soap
always the scum floated to the top

Substitute Teacher
or
The morning Billy Klogphorne taught the adolescent male Sunday School
class lesson on the designated Christian Leader Preparation
outline topicof Genesis 5: 18, 19 and 23, 24,
proving Lamech and polygamy were of the lineage of
Cain and therefore accursed of God
and
Why he was never invited back
to teach Sunday School again

Boys
or should I say young Christian Leaders
potential Deacons of God's true church
I have little to say regarding today's topic
not being familiar with canonized rites of exegesis
therefore this may be a brief experience
in fact the following is potentially the sum of what
I have to say on the matter of Lamech and his wives

Bigamy or polygamy is a crime
That is a fact upon which I will briefly postulate
In a terribly over-populated world it is an inexcusable act
of poor manners, selfishness and stupidity
I do not know if it is a sin
but I cannot imagine or countenance
believing in a Texan god who would condone
much less encourage it
or a Texas woman who would tolerate it
That is my analysis and opinion

Brother Klogphorne
isn't it adultery? and isn't adultery a sin?

Young man
that is a wholly different topic
but in any case I do not believe it is necessarily so
Adultery is recreation
however, it is dangerous contact sport
recreation practiced by all of humanity
normally based upon a lie and because of the lie
it may or not be sin

Brother Klogphorne
isn't lying a sin?

Not always young proselyte
There are categories of both sin and lie
to which all poets and piddlers are exempt
by fact of diplomatic and professional immunity
and all politicians guilty
the divisions being first malicious
and then those designed to prolong one's life, sacrosanct idleness
marriage or commerce with teenage progeny
which should be automatically forgiven
but not so the malicious
which are lies designed to inflate the self like a toad
or tear down another person like a glow worm
deliberately crushed beneath a miscreant's heel
in order to take away or mar what is rightfully his
or in some instances hers

Brother Klogphorne, then what is sin?
the ones they say you can go to Hell for?

Well sir young believer
while Brother Dante Alighieri who well may
have preached a revival service at this edifice some time in the past
did a remarkable job of stratifying hell-bound sin

I will offer the following as my personally updated
Texas-based additional considerations
The only sins you can go to Hell for from any god I could believe in
are murder of one who did not need killing
stealing something of value or precious memory from someone who
needed it, fraud on the part of politicians and currency manipulators
provocations of any war without the intent
of taking an active role in the actual combat effort
that being overt cravenness
and then the ones you're familiar with from this training
designed to produce the next generational crop of deacons
and elders including not being a tithing member
of whoever's church you're talking to
having sex with children
dancing for Baptists and Campbellites
the latter for which it is the Unforgivable Sin
not putting enough money in the collection plate
and malicious and political lying

all others are recreational and forgiveable
or just bad manners
which is why we have wives
to affect and inflict punishment

You don't think adultery
and fornication are sins
then?

I believe I have covered that topic
as well as I am able
the remainder is the parental responsibility
based on familial more' and obfuscation
What else can I do for you young potential missionaries?

Mr Klogphorne
can I ask you a personal question?

Of course you may
I am all rimed ears
so you fire away

Did yall have sex
when you were alive back then?

Young man
this being inside a churchhouse
I am bound by oath, covenant, and custom
to tell the truth, the whole truth
and nothing but the truth
so here it is complete and intact
We invented sex

It did not exist prior to our discovery
the world being dystopic and non-functional
My generation gave our youth wholeheartedly
to the definition, methodology and perfection of the practice
up to the point that it exists today
which is the legacy of trust we pass on to you
for final realization and fulfillment

If any of you have doubts whatsoever
as to the veracity of that statement
ask your parents or grandmothers
and I promise you this
Your parents will look you directly in the eye
and lie to you about the subject
as a matter of sacred protection of our mutual trust secrecy
regarding divine inspiration and creation
and your grandmothers will blush and deny that sex exists at all
then go sit somewhere in the cool shade
with a purloined Baby Jesus fan
wondering whatever possessed you to ask such a thing

and that will be your unimpeachable proof
mark my words

Brother Klogphorne
do you remember when you learned about it?

Young fellow sir neophyte
I most certainly do
every one of you in this room should know Maxine Durrant
and if you have not been in her Woman's Store
to buy your mother a birthday present
I am ashamed of, with, by and for you
as she was the most beautiful young creature
in the world since Eve when we were going
about the business of inventing sex
I coveted her as not one of but The pearl of great price
much to my avail as she had little libidinous interest in me
to my great wonder and misfortune
I will divulge this as my incidental role
in the Creation of Sex for the first time in public
She could have read me
the Tale of the Destruction of Sodom and Gomorrah
or the genealogical begettings of the antediluvian patriarchs
and I would have got a hard on

Now as a result of your silence
I assume you have no further questions this morning

Mister Klogphorne
is that where the story my daddy tells
about your stob came from?

Young reverend
I did not know that event had trickled down
like the understanding of federal taxes
to the ears of Garza County Republican youth

I am embarrassed it has come to you
in a potentially contaminated form
therefore I will tell you the entire veracious rendition
of that epic tale complete and unembellished

I was in Maxine Durrant's store purchasing a transparent negligee
for my wife's recurrent twenty-ninth birthday
with expectations of forthcoming exhibition and rejoinder
when Miss Durrant made a comment upon the low riding condition
of my trousers saying I believe verbatim, Billy
one of these days your britches are going to fall down to your knees
I can't imagine what holds them up
whereupon I in Biblical language divinely inspired saith unto her
Maxine, of all people on earth
I would have thought you would know
I have a stob that holds them up
since you are the one who made me aware of it

What happened then
Mister Klogphorne?

Why of course
without further ado she took my money, gift wrapped the package
in a manner harbingering pomp and circumstance
and upon my leaving locked the door, pulled down the shades
and I would fervently wish declared first call
then poured herself a libation before Aphrodite
At least I have faith and hope that is factual
Is there anything else?

Brother Klogphorne
who was Lamech?

Who was Lamech?
Young Master Ivins of the whiplash Epimethian focus
you will need to ask your grandparents

as those legendary citizens from these parts
probably knew him
since he lived over to Justiceburg
as they might say in unspoiled Texanese

Lamech lived at Justiceburg?
Texas?

Young fellers
Acolytes Nutt and Newberry I believe
who do you think wrote the Bible?
Haven't you heard of Eden
and Palestine, Texas? Titus, Trinity and Godley counties?
The Bible was written by, for and about people
not just made up nonsense dictated out of thin air
Of course Lamech Johnston lived out south of Justiceburg
married Rayola Owens and then
Pearl Rae Higgins of the substantial bosoms
after her mama threw her out of the house for stealing
the secret of her daddy's almost perfected perpetual motion machine
and pouring out his bootleg intended home brew,
a moral and conspicious crime which earned for them the reward
of all consequent affliction and reprobation
upon which they moved to the sanctuary of Utah
somewhere west of Eden near a town originally called Hurry Cain
named after his grandfather of preceding generations
who had to rush all the way there to escape
Texas Rangers' vengeance after killing his brother
for stealing a sheep he loved in the custom they knew unto then

you can read about it
in an early edition of the Garza Dispatch
if you follow the scriptures and search out
matters of truth with fear and trembling
in a plain manner of allusionary speaking
But now I see our allotted time is up

so you gentlemen will be needing to depart
and hear words of wisdom
from our beloved pastor the Right Reverend Strayhorn
As my conclusion I fervently hope I have given you young elders
something to ponder over this morning

Brother Klogphorne
we always end our class with a prayer
would you offer it?

Well Lord up there wherever
to say it delicately and in trochaic synesthesia
I certainly hope it was larded odoriferous
with the septical fragrance of churchhouse proselytization
that will linger in these boys' memory for up to nine seconds
then flow down to this community
unadulterated and abridged for time immemorial
and if that is the resultant actuality
I will leave this earth a delighted and thankful man
Amen

Now you boys have yourselves a real nice Sunday
endeavoring to persevere in the effort
not to squirm or squiggle in your pews
but give your devoted attention to matters
of behavioral hegemony and high consequence

*   *   *

Did you understand that? said Roy Don Staples
I didn't understand nothing
but that part after Sodom and Gomorrah said Jarvis Griggs
It's Sunday School, you're not posta understand it yet said Bobby Hudman
I don't think it was pure scriptural said Charles Ivins
How do you know? said Walter Bloodworth
I know it in my heart said Charles Ivins

You don't know Jack Shit said Monroe Newberry
You caint say that in the churchhouse said Roy Don Staples
Nah uh said Monroe Newberry
Yes I do said Charles Ivins

*   *   *

Billy Klogphorne strode
from classroom to apse to
aisle to mispronounced foyer
through the church house front door
drove home without an acknowledgment
of sermon or scripture or hymnsinging or prayers
or communion or mandatory collection plate passage
his job as substitute Sunday School mentor and Professor
completed indubitably terse, thorough and Texas true
his lesson to the male youth of Garza County taught
his etched inscription into the permanent memory
of our community established satisfactorily
finally, indelibly, permanently
once and by god for all

amen

Lost in Translation
a monologue from the pickup cab

That year I'm thinking about
the popular bubblegum set-in-Italy
movie of the season had Troy Donahue
having overthrown and tossed away
Sandra Dee with the summer's morning garbage
a venal and moral sin of an unforgivable nature
to the unsophisticated and uninitiated
post-pubescent likes of moi, in which he,
courting unabashedly Suzanne Pleshette
I believe, and whilst so doing
used the term *al di la* Troy-translated
as *beyond the beyond* that being I suppose
a Swahili or Reformed Egyptian term of endearment
certainly not Italian or technical Romantic
upon finding the current operable
teenage love of a lifetime
with such linguistic power it secured
an immediate and for some Young Republicans
lifetime addiction to the expression
so that:
        every Texas girls' 1962 high school annual
was signed *All de Lah* by the current
or aspiring suitor to which there was a clamor
of tearstruck emotional overthrow
at any female suitee gathering of the clavern
for purposes of stratification alignment
of eternal phylogynous commitment with an expiration warranty
of 1 June, some assembly required
by all those both signed and unsigned in that manner

which:

        directly leads me to the matter
of contemporary reflective personal poignancy
ergo my undeclared adoration that very season
for the senorita bonita Eva Saenz
to and for whom I refused usage of *al di la*
already in my self-proclaimed maturity
deemed trite to the shaven rimrock of cliché
whereupon I cast about for an appropriate
foreign, exotic and to the 10th power romantic
term of endearment
                  but
having poor personal macaronics in my equipage
I by force of choice turned to a source
of higher wisdom upon which and whence
I trundled to my friend and her brother Gabriel Saenz
who suspected my infatuation with the lovely Eva
and queried him for the exact Spanish or Mexican
poetic maxim I should use to win
her undying love for a lifetime
                      upon which
he told me not *te quiero* as that profession
must come much later after I had secured her heart
but that the *te* and familiar tense would certainly
create an atmosphere of reciprocity
                      therefore
after a long eight seconds spent in heavy ponderation
he opined
        I will give you an amorous expression
steeped in the art of courtly love
Andreas Cappelanus notwithstanding
guaranteed to create Love's flight straight to her soul
but
        you understand these words must never
be spoken in daylight and always
                    whispered

sotto voce softly and distinctly into her ear

                                        as I recall
and I said Fine, give it to me right now, I'm primed
and he said
                In a loving voice gently murmur
tu eres una pendeja and your words
will strike her heart like St Teresa's
flaming arrow of lightning
                            perhaps
the truest statement uttered on this planet
since the Sermon on the Mount

as Eva
            upon hearing my love psalm
turned directly and with her soft hand
folded into a love knot like she held
a roll of dimes for tithing
                            smat me a lick
whose smiting resounded as thunder
to shake Mr. Milton's throne of heaven

it was two years before she spoke
to me again and a year after that
before I found out what her sonofabitching brother
invoked upon me, an event perhaps seminal
in the focus of our lives, perhaps all for the better
as we were doomed at best to be star crossed lovers
between eras of acceptability

and now with Marvell's winged chariot at my back
I can only turn to the marvelous Mr. Nims
for solace
            It was love lost
        And a year lost of the few years we
                Account most

truly beyond the beyond in the language of recuerdos
and adoration, a mental hiatal hernia
that being pretty much all I have to say
on that subject for the time at hand
so I'll ask you not to bring up the tragic matter again
just drive the hell on, paisano, see
if you can find us a back road
where we can stop to bleed our lizards
and then carry on toward the coming of the night

Second Visitation

You won't sell it to me
can I come look at it?

Anytime

Any?

Yep

All right then

Prelude to the World's Greatest Meatloaf Sandwich

Billy on a loquacious backroad beatup Dodge pickup day proclaimed:

the current mode of intellectual meandering
evidently modeled upon the trilogy or triptych
that being the full much ado length and breadth
of the average politician's remembrance
or number of words he can clearly inscribe
upon the indigent palm of his left hand
or write on a note card with crayon

therefore I shall appropriate the format of favor
in order to introduce my current universe trembling
trinity of fears and speculations without development
or undue and unnecessary political commentary
followed by the day's overwhelming question
hence I shall proceed with a postulation:
behold my nominations for the two greatest
potential evils our society faces today
those being the threats of anorexia and
exercise addiction against which I daily strive
to arm myself and fight the good fight
a battle in which I am proud to claim temporary victory

followed by my greatest personal psychological fear
namely acrophobia, an advanced paranoia
that preoccupies me daily as I watch
Willy John climb his sculpture like a fucking
derrick monkey and no matter how I turn
he seems a half slip from plunging oblivion
to the point that my terror has become my nemesis
having chosen my dreams in which to live

and lastly, as I have neither faith, use for, nor belief
in theological anthropomorphism, I have taken exactly that
as a topic for intensive thought, study, and speculation
since my recent visit to Big Bend Park
produced one predominating conundrum, namely
how many thrones do these desert gods need?

That's it? said Clovis

The magic number being accomplished, can there be more?

That is the overwhelming question?

Most certainly not, paisano

What must it be then, Mr. Eliot, I presume?

The overwhelming question of the day
which in this instance you must answer is
where do you propose to drive this goddam truck
to a full stop so we can step out
and consume us some lunch?
Can you handle that magnificent interrogative, sirrah?

I shall put mind, body, and perhaps non-existent soul to the task
and I scuttle to do so
meanwhile pondering the depth of your proclivity

Hear hear, well assessed my Yorick
let us make haste to the appointed hour

Hark, my genius of the armadillos
before us I see Miss Lela's Dew Drop Inn
the winged chariot draws near

Idyll

From the lunch counter at the Dew Drop Inn
while one customer visited the lavatory

Yeah, Clovis had this dog
that had the habit of running off
and then getting lost
so many times

his wife changed its name
from Ivan Doig
to Ubi Sunt

so he'd quit asking
every other day
where'd that sonofabitch go
this time?

he can explain in a minute
the why and wherefore
if you ask, yeah

Pain

Now how'd you do that? said John
and Clovis told him
about the pickup being stuck
wouldn't start
how he got mad and put his back
against the front and started it rocking
then gave all he had
heard the discs rupture
even before the blue pain
picked him up and threw him
on the ground
eyeball to antenna with a red ant
that crawled up his nose
and he didn't care

I've never hurt that way Clovis said
it was the worst pain a man could feel

Oh shit said John it is not
is it Billy?
you lain back down right now
how'd you like it if I taken
and pult on these tractor ropes
they got you hooked up to
wouldn't that hurt just as bad
or worst?
and what if that one fat nurse
name Martha Rae come in
pull down your covers
with her crapper pan again
says Lift up you gotta try some more

staring at you and you aint got
no underwears on?
you gone tell me that don't hurt some?

and everbody come in
says Well that aint so bad
mine was worst
or My brother he torn his back up
like yours and he still caint walk
or His pecker still don't have no feeling
in it and that was twenty years ago
or the doctor come in
says We gone have to operate on you
and everybody you known
says Don't let him cut you
you'll be cripple for life
their uncle he's in a wheelchair
ever since caint do nothing
slobbers down the front of his shirt
nothing below his neck works
all the doctor's fault
you won't never be the same no more
you gone tell me that aint the worst
to hear truestories like that
and you just laying on your butt
in the bed taking up space
from people that's really sick

no that aint the worse
it aint even the worse I heard of
I'll tell you about some pain

everybody knows about that feller
set down on a crapper
at Possum Kingdom Lake

got blackwidow spider bit
on his privates and the whole end of it
come off with the poison
but I known a man
had cancer in the mouth
hurt so bad he chewed
half his tongue off before he died
got blood poison and gangrene
anothern had to chop his leg off
with a hatchet to get out
of a beartrap or he'd froze to death
died anyway in a car wreck
going to his mother's funeral
a year later so it wasn't worth it
and old Dan Walker
when his tractor wouldn't start
hit it with a sledgehammer
missed and broke his shinbone
crawled a mile to his house
and they'd unhooked his phone
because he's behind on the bill
that's pain

but they's some
kindly hurts a different way
sometimes even worse
it was this boy in the fifth grade
who was being called Johnny Mendietta back then
he would of stoled his daddy's pickup
given it to you
for this one little girl name Danella Hagins
to say hello to him
but he's a Mexican and that's too bad
for him back then
so he helt it in all year

here comes Valentine Day
what'd he do? goes down
to Bob Collier drugstore
taken and bought her a box
of red Valentine candy and a card
given it to her at the class party
we all remembered
because she cried and had to go
to the nurse's office
she's so embarrassed to have a Mexican
do such a thing to her
he never come back to school
the rest of the year
I think that hurt pretty good

that aint the worse
I known of
I hurt just as bad
over Thelma Lou Shackleford
when I's seventeen
we all went out to eat fish
we'd been messing around all day
it was that night I known
I loved that girl more'n life
we all order oysters and horse relish
except Thelma Lou
she orders catfish and the man
says You want that broil or fried ma'am?
she said Fried
I can still hear the way that sound
slid off the front of her tongue
I's so ashamed eating raw oysters
I couldn't hardly hold one
in my mouth and Tommy Wayne Clayborn
ate his and half of mine

slopped saurcet all over the table
like a hog licking his fingers
I watched her eat every bite
of her fish begging myself John
ask her to go for a ride
but I's too ascaired
afraid she might say no or laugh
when she's through
Tommy Wayne says Come on Thelma Lou
let's go up Sawmill Road
she never said a word
got up and walked off with him
it wasn't nothing I could do
but watch her go

and that's not the worse
Thelma Lou was my sister's bestfriend
I known for a fact
because Thelma Lou told her
and sworn her to a life secret
so she told me
how when she's twelve and come in
first time how she never known
what it was
nobody done told her
she thought she's busted something
bleeding to death
she went in the kitchen
told her mother
her mother never turnt around
said You get out of this room
you shut the door behind you
caint you see I'm cooking supper?
I think that's worse

but even worst than that
was Tommy Wayne Clayborn
knocked her up and I think he done it
that night I couldn't say nothing
on the Sawmill Road
they didn't know what to do

everybody in town known about it
before they got around to telling their folks
finally Tommy Wayne told
his daddy name Shirley Clayborn
he's the sheriff back then and a good one
about the toughest man in town
partly because of his name
you'd say Morning Shirley
he'd look right in your eye
if it was sparkling any
it wouldn't be purdy quick
so Tommy Wayne told him
he said What you gone do, boy?
Tommy Wayne said Gone marry her, Daddy
Shirley said Is that what you want?
Tommy Wayne said Yas she's a hell of a girl
and she was goddammit
Shirley Clayborn called her family over
they all talked it out and said okay
if that's how it is
and nobody got his ast kicked
like he should of
when they left Tommy Wayne
was just standing there in the room
with his daddy
Shirley went over and poured
two glasses of bootleg whiskey
he'd confisgated out said You want a drank?

Tommy Wayne said Yas I do, I think
and they did
then Shirley Clayborn said
Boy, do you know what's worst
than doing what you did to that girl
in the backseat of my Chevrolet car?
and he said No Daddy, what?
Shirley Clayborn said
Not doing that to that girl
in the backseat of my Chevrolet car
and that's pain.
All my life I've had to known
I never had a daddy like that
and it aint no way I know how
to be one either
and you caint tell me you hurt worst
than I do about that

and besides
I busted my back up
like yours
and I think mine's worst
when I got home
I couldn't set up in bed by myself
so LaVerne she put a screw in the ceiling
we hooked up a comealong
to help me get up and a belt around my chest
so I needed to pee and I hit that ratchet
belt slipped down around my belly
I done comealong my back up off the bed
I holler and here comes LaVerne
she don't know how to undo
that ratchet and let me down
she hits it three licks there I am
my head and feet touching the bed

and the rest of me
pretending to be a rainbow with slipped discs
me needing to pee
the only way she could think of
to get me down so I'd quit hollering
was with a hacksaw
neighbors a mile off heard me and come down
fore she got me cut aloost
seen where I couldn't help it
peed all over my bed
I couldn't do nothing but lay in it

so don't tell me or Billy about no worst pain
because it aint never the worse
it's always something better'n that
you can bet on it anyday
besides, here come the fatnurse
so you better be getting ready, now.

Lake Hills, Texas
A Tale of Rapunzel's Lover

Once in his mind
an open window
moonflooded
upon a sweat and sex stained
flat twin bed
sheet curtain
>   *made at Postex Cotton Mill, Texas*
>   *and shipped to J. C. Penney*
>   *in San Antonio*

paflumped its belly
against blacksnake wind
crawling forty years backward
into the tornado crazed
Algerita Hotel bedroom
of his darkest memory
>   *you just bed not go back in that place again*
>   *she might be Eve in the garden*
>   *or that Lilith or mebbe the bruja they say*

even though he knew
he would find his way
through the nightmare maze
many times
to learn if the story's end
might change
>   *she beside him*
>   *lying upon a moon shard*
>   *in the Duffy Hotel in Bandera*

instead of locking him outside
her mind's door
where he stands, still
trying to find a way
to get back
into his

        even now
        even then
        after all that

Zen and the Art of German Engineering

1

For his 74th birthday
Charles E. Carr, Sr. the Second

received fifteen dollars in the mail
with a handscribbled signature
inside a Judy's Motel notepad tear away
from your son Charles E. Carr, Junior III.

which burned an archetypal hole
in his proverbial pocket

until he went
to Hamilton Drug Store
found the Braun Electric Dry Razor
he'd heard about on radio and t. v.
said How much is it?
Gordon Hamilton said Seventeen seventy-five

Holy cow he said
I bought a Remington
out the Sears catalog
for six dollars
not that long ago

That would have been in 1936
said Gordon Hamilton
the cheapest model
I got one, too
and it wasn't worth a damn
these ones are good
made all the way over to Germany

I only got fifteen dollars
said Charles E. Carr, Sr.
Gordon Hamilton said
I'll think about it
come back and see me this afternoon

Charles E. Carr, Sr.
drove to Bill Edwards Hardware and Appliance
two blocks away
said Can you order me
a Braun Electric Dry Razor?
Bill Edwards got his book out
said Yes I can
it'll be sixteen dollars and fifty cents
including shipping
be here next Tuesday
Charles E. Carr, Sr. said
I'll think about it
get back to you this afternoon

drove back to Hamilton Drug
said Gordon, Ign get that razor
down to Bill Edwards
for under sixteen dollars
Gordon said Is that right?
Charles E. Carr, Sr. said Yep
though I'd of rather do bidness
with you being a neighbor
but I still only have fifteen

What if I sell it to you for fifteen fifty?
What if Bill Edwards went to fifteen?
I'll go fifteen and a quarter, no less
yougn get a quarter from your wife
I can?
Yep

How'd you know that?
What if I called and asked her?
You didn't do that
What if I did?

Can you gift wrap it?
It's a birthday present

2

On the morning after his 74th birthday
Charles E. Carr, Sr. the Second
broke out in a blood bright rash
head to neck
down his shoulders, arms
scratched himself raw and moaned
like a three tawn cat in heat

his wife
stuffed him in the Buick
drove to Dr. Tubbs

You got shingles
said the Dr.

Is it some pills I can take for it?
said Charles E. Carr, Sr.

Yessir, but it's going to take some time
said Dr. Tubbs

How much?

Dollars or time?
You're going to be taking penicillin
and administering calamine lotion

for at least a month
on all afflicted areas
including some you might not
know about yet

Month?

Yessir and I hope your missus
will come to enjoy your looks
because you're going to get downright scruffy
not being able to shave the whole time

3

Forty days forty nights
Charles E. Carr, Sr. the Second
lived in his Barcalounger
memorizing the schedule
of every program on Channel 7 and 11
Ding Dong School with Miss Francis
Captain Kangaroo soap operas all the days of his life
Queen for a Day Hopalong Roy Gene Durango Kid
Cisco and Lone Ranger Howdy Doody
Liberache and Tennessee Ernie Ford oh my both ways
Serenaders at 5 Bernie Howell on the Organ at 5:30
Douglas Edwards Edward R. Murrow See It Now
Jimmy Issac's State News and Weather from Lubbock
Father Knows Alfred Hitchcock Best Loretta Young
Ed Sullivan Loves Lucy Milton Berle
Sid Caesar Dizzy Dean Dragnet Gunsmoke
It's after eleven o'clock
will you turn that goddam thing down?

Yes dear I wished you wouldn't talk that way

I'm getting real tired of this I'm warning you

Yes dear

his scruff sprouting through
a peat moss mask of dried pink lotion
splotches and patches
in his lap every day, all night
his Braun Electric Dry Razor
which during every commercial
sunrise to midnight, forty consecutive days
in the wilderness of temptation
he would lift, hold before his face
thumb the switch
after checking that the cord was plugged in correctly
and listen to its perfectly engineered
immaculately designed
happy birthday from your son Charles E. Carr, Jr.
impeccable German whine

The Second Miracle

Daryl Glen Strickland
ten years into his current drunk
found his way to the monument
with a Jax beer in one hand
the remaining three of the six pack
papersacked in the other

looked up at the sculpture
the seeming spiral movement
the face changing expression
with the light flow, sift of breeze
passing through the welded body
dizzied him
until he dropped to a knee
where he remained for a quarter hour supine
staring upward into the obelisk
then rose and stumbled to the garbage barrel
tossed in his open can
placed the three live soldiers beside the drum

that night at the Dew Drop Inn
Bus Pennel mentioned
the Monument to the South Plains
Daryl Glen Strickland once again
wobbled until he had to leave the bar
go outside for fresh air
from then on when he came
to the Dew he drank only R.C. Cola

he returned again and again
to view Willy John's first masterpiece
sober

saying any time he thought of drinking
he pictured it in his mind
and dizziness poisoned the urge

said he was pretty sure
he overheard himself
praying to it a few times
until he finally gave it up
for good

the men's glee club at the Dew Drop
said Poor devil
he's cursed with the genius
caint get it out of his system
probley rurnt forever
they said
That's too bad
he was a good old boy
oncet upon a time

Eloise Ann's Story:
Upon Her Daughter Finding the Shotgunned Bodies
of a Sandhill Crane and her Colt
in the Grainfield Stubble

I remember when I was her age
one of our neighbors shot my puppy
Daddy said He will pay for that in the hereafter
down the road from our place
somebody had painted on a sign

REPENT
JESUS IS COMING
SOON
THE END IS NEAR

and I thought then
no it isn't
either it's already come and gone
and He went away, left for good
or it's too late
we are all sunsucked dry with meanness
where a bucket of water on cheatgrass
wouldn't pull enough suption
to let a stem call up spit

why would He want to come back to this?
that's what I wanted to know
what I had to say about all of it back then
when I was a child like her wondering
why somebody would do something like that
to my puppy dog, to me
to my whole world and everything
I'd learned to believe in
about it all

The Committee to Review and Revise
The Board of Education Mission Statement

This little light of mine
—Vacation Bible School song

You put me on that committee
first thing I'll do is call a vote to disband

Is it the committee or the people on it?

It's about equal, I'd guess

Is there anything today you detest more than educationists or committees?

Probably prayer before the meeting starts

You don't approve of praying

Not in public, nosir, but that's not the point

What is then?

Praying before an education meeting is akin to beseeching omnipotent
permission
in this instance to enact revisionist precepts of the moronic and mundane
a silly concept for which I have neither patience, respect nor time of day
I would rather proceed without same then ask forgiveness for idiotic
transgression
which is a Christian, even a Baptist Christian, obligation to remit
The people on that committee are too intellectually rigid to even
            acknowledge that

I see what you mean

I accept that analysis maintaining reservations

It's not a big deal anyway, Billy, being more figurehead than reality
I doubt that committee even has the authority to disband itself

Full circle, full cliché
if nominated I will not run, if elected I will not serve
being unwilling to lead or follow in this meaningless matter
I move to cease discussion and approve my stance by acclamation
that movement being neither debatable nor amendable

I second that motion and vote yea

That, sir, being a highly commendable votive castureation worthy of one PBR

Which I accept with honor

Let us go then you and I
while the evening spreads against the sky
like alcoholics to the School Board Meeting

I, sir, am not an alcoholic
I am a votive casturationist drunk

The difference being?

Alcoholics go to meetings
I'm going to Adolph's

Perhaps you do know Jack Shit
and in that light
I, sir, will be your Sancho Panza

Let's shine, compadre
stars aglitter in mud puddles
let us go forth and shine

Higher Authority

Oh Hell! what do mine eyes with grief behold?
—*Paradise Lost* IV, 360

1

What are you doing!
Oh god
Oh shit
Jimmy Don who is that in my
     Kim Pierce! What are you
I can explain Mrs Strachioner
No you can't
Oh god
Young lady you get out of my bedroom
Baby, I can
Don't you Baby me   Get out of my bed
    that piece of flesh you're with is a high school student, a minor
    you should be really Really ashamed of yourself
    you concubine chasing scum sucker child molesting snotty nosed Poland
    China boar hog
    I don't want to ever see you again
       Really, I can
Don't you say another word, Miss Pierce
    you get your clothes on
    and yourself out of my house
Oh shit
And I can tell you one more thing, young lady
    you are getting an unexcused absence
    for this
Oh Hell! There goes my reputation
Baby, we can work this out
No we can't, we won't

get your clothes on
          both of you get out of this house
If this gets around I'm dead
          Jerry Tey will ask
          for his class ring back, I know it
Get out of this house Now
Baby, you need to set down
          and think this over
Jimmy Don, you have one minute
          to be out of this house
          I'm getting the shotgun
          and I won't be particular
          about where I'm aiming
Oh god
You have 54 seconds left
Oh shit, I think she means it
Oh god
50 seconds
          I know where it is and it's loaded
I'm leaving, I'm leaving
You don't have any clothes on, Kimmie
You can go fuck yourself, Mister Strachioner
          I'm not getting shot over this
44
Baby
42
I'm out
          I'm out
          just settle down
38

2

Elder Ezell when I was a little girl
back when you were only a Deacon
Mama always told me you were our friend
the one person I could come to and trust if I had a bad problem
to listen and help me through it
if they were gone or if I thought they couldn't help
besides going to the preacher

I don't know Brother Ronnie Parker
that well yet he's too new to the church
I wouldn't feel comfortable
going to him even if he is our Minister
will you hear me as my Elder and my friend
and offer any advice you have on what to do next?

Your mama was Maypearl Fleming wasn't she?
married to Floyd Fleming before he died
when? back in '54 I think?
wasn't it a heart attackt back then?

Yes sir

You're Lucy Beth Strachioner now aren't you?
married to Jimmy Don Strachioner who works
up to Brown Brothers as a oiler, don't he?
secretary to the Principal down to the high school I believe?
do I got that right?
Jimmy Don he's not a member of the Church is he?

Yes sir and no sir, he's a Baptist
that's exactly right

Well what is it I can do for you today Miss Lucy Beth?

85

Elder Ezell
this is the hardest story of my life so far to tell
and I don't know rightly how to do it
so I'll just start before the beginning actually was

It was dinnertime yesterday
all the kids out to eat and drag main
I had some time before the afternoon bell rang
thought I'd run some errands go to the Post Office maybe the bank
I went out to the parking lot to get in my car and do them
but it wouldn't start
It wouldn't run at all
I went back to see if anybody could help
but the whole building was empty and the phone system down
the only thing I could do was walk home to see if Jimmy Don
could come help me get it running if he was there
that's over half a mile

when I got home it looked like nobody else was
then I heard this noise from the back
when I went to see he was there Jimmy Don
and this high school girl with a terrible terrible reputation
in our bed naked as the day they were born
coupleating right in front of me
I was so shocked I didn't know what to do
I have no idea what I said or did but I threw them both out
and told Jimmy Don he shouldn't never come back again
but he finally did that night anyway

he tried to explain it all away
I didn't let him
I got the facts and the matter of it is
he and that Kim Pierce child

Walter and Mary Dell Pierce's girl

Yes sir, that one
they've been carrying on that way
ever since Charles Huffman's homemade Halloween
Horror Show back in October in our house right in my bed

I seen her there that night selling tickets said Johnny Bert Ezell

He said he was sorry and would try to make it up to me
I told him to pack up his clothes go find somewhere else to live
with his little high school extracurricular activity
whose tardys I'd changed every one to unexcused absences
now that I knew what she'd been doing all these months
during 5th period Homemaking Class
he said he didn't have anywhere to go
besides she'd already told him it was over between them
she'd even got her boyfriend to understand
and forgive her concubinal behavior
so why wouldn't I do the same thing for him
as my Christian duty to be a subservient wife
he slept on the couch by himself last night

I know divorce is not appreciated by the Church of Christ
but what am I supposed to do?
I feel wronged
dirty
forsaken
cheated upon
adultered
and mocked in the eyes of my community
he won't agree to go before his church or mine
and beg forgiveness
he says it is none of anybody's business
it is my duty as his wife to get over it and get on with our lives
just the way it used to be

I do not believe I can do this, Elder Ezell
I believe I have to end either my marriage
or my life
I am so ashamed and embarrassed
filled with anger and even hatred
I don't know what to do
I don't even know if I can go back to work
I don't know if I can attend church services
I am so ashamed of it all
that's why I came to you

Do you think you can kindly help me any?

3

Lucy Beth
when a car won't start
the first thing I'd do was check the fuel gauge
turn on the key and if the line don't come up
it's probley out of gas and that's your problem

if there's gas I'd raise the hood
and look over the front down to the fuel filter
if the glass bowl is empty it's probley a clogged intake line
if it isn't see if it's cloudy or has foreign matter globules
yougn unhook the bottom line and drain it off
air bubbles is more for vapor lock than starting
but you can tap them away most times with your pocket knife

if that's not it I'd say it will be a matter of ignition or combustion
I'd start with the battry
check the poles and connections first then take off the caps
see if any cells is dry and fill them with clean water if it is
then jump start or charge
I'd recommend 2 amp 72 hours for complete build up

was the red light shining on the dash controls?
it could be the generator, check the belts
if it's the brushes yougn get a set at Bill Edwards Hardware and Appliance
just take the old ones out the new ones will go right in the clips
it's real simple if you know how to do it

when you tried to start it did it turn over or was it flat line
or went Clunk? that could be the solenoid
you should of turned the key over and over oncet at a time
to see if the forks might come down and engage
but you may need to crawl under and get it off
the top of the starter where it sets
might pay you to take the starter off while you're at it
get it tested out yougn get a rebuilt one at Bill Edwards
or a junker out to Charley Baker's wrecked car lot
be careful of him selling you trash he knows won't work

now if it's a matter of combustion
I'd start the easiest with the sparkplugs
pull any one out with your socket-ranch
give it a look to see if it's foult
you'll know it in a instant when you look
some file and sandpaper then airblow them
I'd just get a new set down to Bill Edwards
don't get no dadgum Champions get AC's
they're worth the extra money
gap them at 32 yougn eyeball it oncet you know what it is

now don't pucker up on me
we're making some headway here
it's just a couple more things to do

go up to the distributor
look over and feel the wores for connection
then take the cap off by pulling out the clips
look over the inside at the rotor and see if its cracked

now bend down over the fender for a sightline
and click the ignition one bump at a time
till the points come all the way open
see if they're flat or ragged
sometimes yougn file that down but if it's burnt
get a new set and put it in just like you took the old ones out
gap it at 17 one thousandths
if that was it that car will start up
and purr like a Siamese kitty cat

I'd still if it was me climb up and screw off
the top of the filter housing and eyeball the air filter
if it's greasey pick it up and feel if it weights heavy
then take and throw it on the ground get anothern and put it in
you'll feel the different right off

Yougn lean over and examine the carburetor when the housing lid's off
I don't recommend you take it off or rebuild it
that's getting a little complicated for a amateur
mebbe take a clean rag if it's hard varnish build up and some solvent
or even turpentine I've heard twicet to get some of it off
you could check the floats and valves and wings and the choke
I don't think it'd pay you to do any more
unless you know what you're doing

you do that and I'll just bet you you've solved your problem
that car will start up and hum like a Esso Bee
but let me tell you this Lucy Beth if it dudn't
yougn bring it right down to the station I'll have a looksee
I'll bet two dollars to a doughnut
wegn get her done one way or anothern

now you cheer up and make a happy face
everything's gone be just all right
that car's gone start up and run real good for you
oncet we get her fixed

4

Earlean!

Yes dear?

Mama, would you come in here
Lucy Beth Strachioner
Maypearl and Floyd Flemingses' daughter
is abawling hysterical and unmerciful
I'm afraid she thinks she's done broke
and rurnt her car
because it wouldn't start up for her
yesterday out to the high school
I've tried to esplain what she could do
but I'm afraid it got too complicated
could you come in here
see if yougn calm her down any
sometimes it takes a womern's touch
to get to the bottom of the problem
that's something I wasn't borned with
this time around
be arunning if you can
I believe she's coming unwound
by the minute

Third Visitation

You know what that needs
is some cattle

Cattle

Tie it to the land, the history

You think

I do
about four mebbe real gentle
grullos and brindles
that would be like pets
oncet you got uster them

Longhorns?

Indigenous
that's a word you said
I like it
mebbe even a old feed lot buffalo
I happen to know where is at
if we was to fence off heavy
around the monument

Buffalo

Add some color
some of that aesthetic value
you educated people talk about

My place is only twenty acres

What if you was to get a lease
on forty more between here
and that cotton field

Forty acres

All right
you're gone press me
eighty then
you strike a hard bargain

Where's all this coming from?

Cattle and buffalo's on loan
I get them back any time I decide
cattle has the original Slaughter brand
so I can prove it
land is a lease

How much lease do you think I can afford?

I'd say upwards of a dollar a year
forty nine years renewable
through Willy John or his legacy
would that do it?

Upwards

Fifty dollars totaled
I'd prefer you pay up front
I don't want no bookkeeping
tying up my valuable time

You sure about this?

Crew'll be out to start on fencing
seven o'clock a.m. in the morning
I expect you ought to be awarning your Missuz
some of them boys can be kindly rowdy
if they don't get morning coffee
like it's supposed to be

Jacks

My granddaughter told me
she was the 4th grade Jacks champion
of her entire school and could hold her own
with most girls and all boys
up through 6th and if I'd like to try her
she'd clean my clock
which she couldn't have done better
with a Brillo pad

while doing Around the Worlds
she informed me it was not a fair contest
as she honestly believed no boy on earth
could touch her unless she cheated down
to make him want to bet on it
said she took Haygood Sojourner's milk money
every day for a week
then heard him saying
he Only let her win because she was a girl
she upped the stakes to 4th grade Championship
of the Known World after school
on the varsity tennis court
so they'd have a perfectly flat playing field
he could bring anybody he wanted to referee or be witness

said she practiced all weekend
got up to Sixies on all variations
where she knew he was dead meat
coming in but to make sure
and Don't tell Mama
she wore her dark blue panties
with bright yellow stars and quarter moons
said I might not know it

but if a girl sits cross legged
when it gets to Pigs in the Pen
and lets her panties show a little
there wasn't any boy up to 7th grade
who could keep his concentration
she took Haygood's milk and lunch money
his Little League medallion on a chain around his neck
spinning top, taw marble, new pencil, ball cap
and his pocket knife he almost bawled over
begged her to get it back
because it was his daddy's
she said she told him Like my Grandpa says
A card laid's a card played
you went double or nothing and lost
so grow up and take it like a man

she knew she could have acted like her elbow hurt
got him to go to a third round
and won his wristwatch
but who wanted it anyway
being a Davy Crockett
but if it'd been Cinderella she'd be wearing it now
she was tired of hearing him whine anyway

she'd set him up in the first game
played like she had a broken wrist
let him get up to Threesies
where he thought he might have a chance
then popped the hammer
said she ate his lunch and then supper
like it was Belshazzar's Feast
including dessert
then put the Handwriting on the Wall
went all the way up to Sixies
before she even let him have a bounce
he didn't make it through Twosies

on Pickups when she pulled her skirt
up to almost her knees to get his mind
completely discombobulated

I asked her if she thought she might ever reconsider
maybe at least give Haygood back the pocketknife
she said No
that was a trophy she intended
to pass down to her children one day
as their inheritance

by then I realized
between sitting on the hardwood floor
and the impossibility of ever doing even Onesies'
Pigs in the Pen much less Double Bouncies
I conceded the match when she passed into Foursies
called Daniel and the Angel to come down
and claim all the credit and glory
to which she said Now, Grandpa,
we have to go double or nothing for keeps
and I said I didn't know we were betting
she said You weren't but I was
I told you my personal championship strategy
and if I win this round
you will have to swear tick a lock secrecy
to never tell it to anybody you can't trust
for the rest of your life
until I get old and graduate from high school
get married and have a baby
when it comes time
to learn Queenship Mastery
you can share it only with her
there are some things a mother
just can't tell a daughter
that's what Grandpa's are for
So get ready Buster

now I'm going to show you
once and for all, no holds barred
how Jacks are played

Elder Johnny Bert Ezell's
Attempt to Re-resign as the Young Adult Men's
Sunday School Teacher

Brother Parker
the Only time in my life
I ever got anything taught
to anybody was when
my boy Charles was six
and on that day I taught him
in one lesson why it's best
not to pick up a cat
by the tail

I've thought hard
and even prayed about it
but I just can't find any way
to bring scripture up or down
to a practical level

From the Pickup Cab on the Back Road to Adolph's

There are a couple of things
about this moving into the golden years
that fall into the category of pesteration

Being?

I can't hear anymore
can't see anymore
can't remember a damn thing anymore
and those are the things that still work

I heard a bad rumor there comes a time
when you give up on the usefulness of memory
but you can designate friends to remember things for you
and when you outlive your friends you'll have your children
but most of all you'll have your wife
to correct and amend all those things you misremembered

I still like it when I can fall
into one of my unadulterated remembrances
and never worry one bit about drowning
or being rescued

Sorta like throwing a rock
through the plate glass window
of your current perception
What's the other botheration?

The fact that on our 50th
the wife asked me if I'd like to come upstairs
we'd try a poke

I had to tell her
anymore I had just enough energy
to do only one chore on a day

Is that a swear-to-god true story?

That question makes me wonder
if I'm the kind of fool you might think I am
and I'm wondering if you've considered
whether or not
you might have misunderestimated me

And I can't remember
far enough back to answer that one

Like another one of my heroes said
Drive for Christ's sake
look out where yr going

Are we there yet?

Nope
but we're gaining

The Third Miracle

Score: South Plains Monument 1: Tornado 0
—Photo caption: *Avalanche Journal*

All night the huge twisters
played hop Scotch and
wreaked mayhem
across the Caprock rim

2:12 a.m.
Willy John snapped the photograph
that graced the Avalanche Journal's
Sunday front page

the sculpture draped
with St. Elmo's fire
around its suppliant base
the cattle's great horns ablaze

from a lightning ravaged sky
like the finger of God
stretched toward the obelisk:
a tornado funnel floating in abeyance

Monroe

Monroe Newberry's life turned on a pivot
the first day of class his fifth grade year
when he met Mr. Byron Edgers
the first male elementary school teacher
in the history of our town
who in order to get to know his class
began the day calling roll backwards
to let them know his class was going to be different
which resulted in him calling Troy Newberry before Monroe
asked him all the appropriate questions
then Monroe next and said
Are yall you and Troy twin brothers then?

Monroe said No
which was about the length of most sentences he spoke
Troy he's almost two years oldern Monroe is, said Butch Bowen
I asked Monroe, not you said Mr. Byron Edgers
let him speak for hisself
how come you're in the same fifth grade class?
Monroe didn't say anything
looked across the room at Troy
who was busy staring out the window
I asked you a question Monroe Newberry
now you have to answer it said Mr. Byron Edgers
Monroe only scrunched his shoulders
Monroe Newberry I axed you a question
he said turning red in the face

Because I failt fifth grade said Troy Newberry
I have to do it over again
which would have been fine except

the whole fifth grade class excepting Monroe
laughed

That's all right hollered Troy
least I'm not a dummy and I've got a man's name Troy
not some movie star womern's name Monroe
Shut up Troy said Monroe
Oh tell everbody how Mama
wanted you to be her purdy little girl
grow up to be all beautiful in the picture shows
had the name Marilyn Monroe Newberry picked out for you
how she'd say You're my purdy little boy
purdy enough to be my purdy girl Marilyn Monroe
Shut up Troy said Monroe
How she brought you a yellar dress
for your third birthday put it on you

Monroe Newberry jumped up
ran over and pulled his brother Troy out of his chair
on the floor his arms swinging like a tilterwhirl
screaming Shut up Shut up
before Mr. Byron Edgers could pull him away
Troy had a bloody nose and a piece of his ear bitten off

then at recess hit him on the side of the head
with Janette Hutto's roller skate
they had to take him to the school Nurse

Mr. Byron Edgers transferred Monroe Newberry
To Gordon Hamilton's wife
Mrs. Johnnie Hamilton's fifth grade section
for the good of the school
Principal Ellis Mills called the daddy
D'Wayne Newberry in to settle it down
Mrs. Newberry already gone
some said dead some said

living with kin in Arkansas some
said in an insane asylum
he said he didn't know what to do
with them boys they was always
at one another one way or the othern
this was the first time he known
Monroe to get the best of old Troy

for the next two years
no one heard a sound from Monroe Newberry's lips
his teachers said he was tongue tied
school Nurse said he was born defected
Principal Mills who was a church Deacon said
It might be the Lord's touch
students and friends knew Monroe was in there
he just wasn't riding the escalator

until the day in seventh grade
when he discovered Hooter Hagin's genuine birth defect
said out loud Jesust Hooter
you only got one tiddy
and the little Dutch boy named Jan
took his finger out of the dike

language began to trickle syllables then words first
few sentences longer than three words
then five
bursts of sudden shyness and reversion
disorientation and confusion
slowly he rejoined us
word by word by sentence by month by day
and then the Saturday
Troy Newberry and his chosen friends and disciples
captured Monroe in his bedroom
told him they were going to find out
if Marilyn Monroe Newberry had a pecker or not

and then maybe cut it off
to see if he'd holler about that at least

screams so loud calls went to the station
and the fire alarm sounded
Deputy Sheriff Junior Shepherd from one side of town
Sheriff Red Floyd from the other
raced the fire truck to the Newberry residence

found four pubescent
hoodlum-in-training eighth grade boys bloody
bruised and battered
scratch and teeth marks asunder
like red silk ribbons flowing in abundance
mauled and abandoned wailing aftermath hog hounds
Troy Newberry nowhere to be found
Monroe in the front yard
holding a broken bed slat in one hand
a ball peen hammer in the other
crowing like a bantum rooster

for the good of the School Board
Troy Newberry was allowed to
drop out of junior high school early
and at the same time take Driver's Training
to get his license on his fourteenth birthday
moved in with his uncle Cephas Bilberry
and took up immediately with his obese Scotch-eyed daughter
Monroe finished the year
graduated from junior high the next

then went off radar
disappearing into the realm of myth and legend
for seven years until someone saw the advertisement
in the Dispatch and elevated it to first page rumor mill status

Notice to all Men 17 or older:
You are invited by your Uncle Sam
to come to the U S Army Recruitment Office
3006 24ᵗʰ Street Lubbock, Texas
see Staff Sergeant Monroe Newberry
to inquire regarding Career Opportunity
under the Guaranteed Europe Enlistment Policy

and even Mr. Byron Edgers
who was by then the Grade School Principal said
at the monthly Board meeting
Well maybe there is a God after all
and a happy ending besides in fairy tales
but who'd a thunk it?
Johnny Bert Ezell
Head of the School Board that night
whispered Good boy
I knew you could do it

Fourth Visitation

Look at that cow groom her calf
that there is a lady of elegance if I ever saw one
and by god knows exactly
what I'm saying about it
don't you, you persnickety senorita bonita

I'd appreciate the hell out of it
you being a man of letters
if you wouldn't repeat the following
until I'm gone
but her name is Juliet

I won't insult you
by mentioning the bull's name
just that this time they made it
unstrangled by their tethers
so what do you have to say about that?

What They Say

When Larry Joe Williams invoked them
that evening at Adolph's Bar and Cafe
Billy Klogphorne rose like Lazarus from his stool
to begin walking with a purpose away somewhere else
to which Larry Joe said Whar you going
I aint finished yet?
so that Billy said to Larry Joe
That's what I feared
but you gave me prologue excuse
I sincerely desired to the point of prayer
Which is what? said Larry Joe
The invocation of an element of imagined society
named They
which does not, has not, and will never exist
but whose ultimate authority referenced gives imprimatur
to proceedence from nonsense through hyperbole
to authentication by summons
of the universal arbiter who will allow the invoker
to propound ideology he does not comprehend
and thereby create pretence of knowledge
emanating from the invented sources ·
he actually on this earth never encountered
nonetheless feels perfectly qualified
to repeat verbatim those elements these ethereal geniuses
of his imagination who incidentally
always happen to agree exactly with him
think, believe, and say to an audience of one

and Billy rising sauntered in search of elsewhere libation
to which Larry Joe Williams opined
What did he say just then
does any of yall known what that was about?

so that Ollie McDougald summarized
To the best of my knowledge
he said They say
you are full of shit
and if that's what they say
I believe it has to be a fact
and that, Larry Joe, is, exactly as they say,
all they are to it

Idyll
Thursday night, Adolph's, Lake Hills, Texas

This is everywhere I've ever been
—John Sims

Do you like being drunk?

Well hell no
where'd you get such of a stupid idea?
I like getting drunk
being drunk isn't much special
getting over being drunk
makes you wonder
why the hell you did that again
but when you start all over
well that's where the difference is

     *   *   *

Heard Jane Lynn she's mad at you

Where'd you hear that at?

Mary Ann

Yeah I trucked in mud
all over the living room floor

She thrown a fit?

She's quiet for a minute
then the lid kindly blew off to hell and back

What'd you do?

Told her I'd get it cleant up torektly
she said Whyn't you try to be honest
just oncet?

*   *   *

Yall hear about Melvin Ray Bird
falling and busting his ribs?

Yeah heard you found him first
what happened?
He was in his pickup all bent over
like he was ahorseback with kidney stones
I said Do you need help?
he said What does it look like to you?

*   *   *

They say now that Odus Millard's dying
he got religion and's making plans
about going to heaven

Being close to death don't mean
you know one goddam thing more
about heaven or hell
than a man who's been married
for fifty years knows about sex
he's trying to remember forward
that never does work worth a damn

*   *   *

Melvin Ray Bird's a tough one

Oh yeah he's tough
got two layers of hard bark on him

that's just the part on his hide

*   *   *

Was he hurt any?

If he wasn't it'll hold him over
till the good hurt comes around

*   *   *

I remember how Odus would set
on his porch furniture awaiting
for whatever might come next
dull as a sop
but alert as a shadebake dog underneath
waiting for any incentive to be abark
any notion come up he could use it as a excuse
for what rurnt his day
I guess I'll miss him anyway

*   *   *

What's a matter his leg?

Aint his laig it's his foot

What's a matter his foot then?

He runned over it widge a wagon

A wagon?

What I said

What'd he do that for?

It's a rolling backards he stuckt his foot out
to stop it and it mashed it

Mashed it widge a wagon

Hauling wood

Godamitey

Mash it flat as a duck

Widge a wagon

Full of forewood

Godamitey

Said it hurt all to hell and his daddy
he had to cut his shoe off his foot

Mashed foot

Widge a wagon

How old?

Bout s'em or nine mebbe back then

Godamitey

Why he limp so bad

I imagine

They lose any wood?

Not that I heard of
his daddy was particular but his mama was pissed off
that shoe'd belong to her brother and it was rurnt

I imagine

You'd be right doing that

Billy you sure been quiet tonight

I'm trying not to explain to myself
but just understand
how a life that long could have
almost no meaning
beyond the immediate fading of memory
even before absence

You're in it pretty deep I'm guessing
a fire burning in your head

Something like having
the beginning part of a definition
hung up in the cross tangled web of a waking dream
without even finding a word it belongs to

That's a little scary, is it?

then it says Here I am
there I was
and precisely what is it
you're planning to do about it?

That's good enough to be quiet about
I believe so
and I believe I won't be saying
There seemed no man
busier than he was
and yet he seemed busier
than he was
with any reference whatsoever to you

who have been wading with hip boots
tonight I believe

It's a little bit like something
one of us might have done
or thought about doing
just exactly over a dozen times at least

That one I agree with

       *   *   *

You drunk enough to soliloquize?

I believe so
What's the topic?

Pick one
R. B. you'n Ollie come on over
Billy's feeling loquacious
maybe even Lucretian
or Menippean

What about?

I expect it will be either the Grand Inquisitor
or the lockbox of creation
or something similar pretentious as hell
it's his speech which he'll deliver unpremeditated
and dictated unimplored by his celestial patroness
whilst slumbering he'll decide

Will we be able to understand it?

Nope, not a word

We'll be right over then

I think I'm thinking about that sculpture Willy John made and how it's wrapped up in time and space. We had to have time and space so we could have a world and live in it. If we didn't have time everything would happen all at once and you'd be your own daddy and son with you smashed and squashed up in between, which, ironically and poignantly, is exactly the way I feel at this particular critical juncture of my near-to-end life, as I constantly feel the press of legacy at my back and my hopes for the future smashed into my face with the mandatory rejection of a considerable portion of my own earned and personal beliefs and ideology by my beloved progeny, all being necessary, intimidating, and, to a somewhat uncomfortable nature that I must come to embrace, repulsive in order to maintain a dynamic world and universe. And if we didn't have space everything would be a swallowing hole with the sun and the moon and every damn one of the stars coming right down on top of us, which, once again, I have come at this juncture to realize is exactly the way I find myself, trapped in a body that is shrinking, crushed, and rotting around me while, in spite of the steady accumulation of evidence to the contrary, I am doing everything possible to maintain a sense of personal strength and dignity whilst living within that confinement, continuing to wage war against the scientific facts of chronology and gravity, fighting the good fight against my persistent fears of exercise addiction and anorexia, yet realizing no longer year by year but week by week at an accelerating pace that ultimately and finally, there is no fucking way I'm even going to win a battle. That's why they are the most important. Without them we wouldn't have Newton's Third Law of Physical Motion. All other things came next, after that. They're all waiting to happen or they've already happened but neither one did until there was a when and a where so it could, and if there wasn't a that, everything immediately becomes a wasn't because there would be no documentation. Thus, it couldn't have been, at least in any objective sense. And that's how his sculpture works for me, with all his assemblage of the paraphernalia of the past thrust up into the ether in a manner worthy of mythological ponderance, what I think it was he was trying to say and how and why it is. So, gentlemen, there you go. All of which

I've come to understand in the course of an evening which has perfectly convinced me that I cannot, should not, and will not ever deserve a claim on any part of that monument or its significance, which in like manner has brought me to the realization that for that very reason the one thing I will desire and lay claim to for the rest of my life is personal aesthetic and enduring mental ownership of that very object, and I've made up my mind that I don't have to think about that any more tonight.

What'd you think, Ollie?

I thought it was purdy good
whatall of it I understood
worth a beer I believe
what about you, Clovis?

It was almost a Stay,
thou art so fair moment
glad I asked for it
In the words of the prophet
I believe we heard
something almost being said
I'm drunk enough to almost shed a tear
over that one

Nope, tears are salty
you have high blood pressure and can't tolerate it
besides it's all gravel road
leading to mere oblivion
let's go home

I like it
sayeth all but Jacques
I'm about ready, Billy
let's call it a quit
and get it over with

John Sims' Story: The Oil Well Fire

Lasciate ogne speranza, voi ch'intrate
—Dante Aligheri, *Inferno*, 111, 9

Don't yall leave yet, come over a minute
and pretend to act like you think
we might actually want you to stay
here, I caint get the top screwt off
this beer I got out of the cold box, Billy
can you or Clovis help?
that's the onliest thing I miss this finger for
I got cut off I just haven't got no grip
to twist off these beer lids
they put them on too tight for me now

they was this guy I heard about
who was a miner or trapper or something
anyways he lived alone up in the hills
I guess mebbe he's a trapper and got it
caught that happens now and then
so he just picked up his finger
stuck it in his pocket and went on home
when he got there he took out his needle and thread
he sewed that finger back on
his hand but it didn't work
two, three weeks later it all swolt up
green and the finger fell off
so's he built a fire in the stove
held the stump agin it
till he burnt all the green poison out
I think a feller'd have to be
pretty much of a man to do that

I knew this other guy loading up
a sow hog and she wouldn't go
he was trying to waller her into the truck
he grabs her by the tail
with one hand, the ear with the othern
she's screaming like hell the whole time

him getting pretty pissed off
he does this a time or two
then grabs her again but
gets the one hand in her mouth
he feels something pinch
pulls back his hand
his finger's gone that damn sow's
bit him off he looked all around
didn't find that finger nowhere
he guessed that sow swallered it

I don't much like to talk about how I lost mine
it still bothers me some
mebbe I'm just too drunk but I started
thinking about it
this all happened before
I went to work for the lectric company
I was younger and hired on for the oil
oh I made good money it wasn't bad work
I don't think I'd do it again
anyways we's up on the panhandle
had a rig drilling about eight miles outa town
we'd work thirty six on and twelve off
at least I would cause I could make so much
I'd run chain awhile and then crow-nest
never made no different
I was just after the paycheck on Fridays
I'd do about anything they wanted as long

as the money kept coming in and they
seemed to like that
anyways we was down over a mile
damn near seven fousand foot
we knew the oil was right there
we had to be coming through any time
you just get the feeling it's gonna blow
here comes the foman cause we sent for him
cause he has to sez when we can cap off
to get ready for the last push through
so we don't blow all to hell and mebbe catch fire
that foman he's so damn drunk
he caint tell dog puke from crap
starts raising all kind of hell saying
You get this goddam rig running right NOW
we won't hit no sonofabitching oil
for two weeks nobody paid you to think
that's what I'm by god paid for
you just drill till I say stop and then
you just ast how long that's all
now get back to goddam work and stop
trying to set round fucking off

he left and we's so mad we couldn't see straight
for a man to talk to us that way
whether he's drunk or not didn't matter
so we set the bit back down in the night
and let her go what the hell

about midnight the crewboss he says to me
John you go up to the crow-nest we lifting
that pipe out I aint getting blowed up
for nobody and that was fine by me
we's all getting ascairt to where we's just working
not saying nothing just thinking
about how long fore morning or till we got off

it's funny how you think the day'll take
the being ascairt away but it never really does
anyways I climbt up the derrick to the top
we's getting ready to pull that pipe out
all of a sudden the whole thing starts shaking
where I'm about to get slung off
I can hear the crewboss yelling
Get down get DOWN this mama's gonna blow
by god I burnt the palms off my hands
coming down I slid the wire guy rope
to the platform and then jumped off on the ground
the rest of the crew's arredy running ahead
so's I try to catch up and then I hear
that big devil's mother touch off K_BOOM
right behind me and caught on fire
it blew me down on the ground and started
me burning by god I was ascairt
I jumped up and started running and I'd of
burnt to death if this man hadn't grapt me
throwed me down in this ditch and
put the fire out on my clothes

so we look and the whole rig's burning
we can see two guys from the crew laying
between us and the rig burning up
we know they's dead
the rest of us burnt bad where we might die
crewboss he takes off running into the fire
we can see he's gonna try to bring the pickup out
he goes to it and grabs the doorhandle
it's so hot part of his hand
sticks to the door and just comes off
but he gets in and somehow
he gets that damn truck started and drives out
of that fire I won't never know how
all the wires was burnt up

it got so hot that truck's paint was all
scorcht off where you couldn't tell
even what kind of a pickup it was
he brings it to us and we get in
I'm so burnt they had to put me in the back
and I'm laying in this feller's lap
who put out the fire in my clothes
we pull out of there driving like hell
was chasing us to get to town
and by then the fire was so hot
it burnt up the whole goddam rig
there wasn't nothing left and I
seen it bend over just like it was plastic
I wanted to pass out so bad I couldn't stand it
I didn't I just laid there and felt it all
and saw it all

so's we're racing the devil to town
as fast as we can go and we pass this law
he turns on his red light and chases us
till he gets close enough to see and then
he pulls ahead and leads us through town
about ninety miles a hour to the hospital
where he jumps out and runs over and opens
the door and he just puked like hell
three up front was arredy dead two of them
stuck together they's burnt so bad
the crewboss's hand was off
he didn't have no face left
how he drove God knows I don't
there was only one othern still alive and
he died that night so then they come
to get us out of the back and they started to lift
me out I said Get him first he saved my life
the man says it's too late he's done dead
I was laying in his lap

onliest two that made it was me and the crewboss
he was in the hospital for ninety six days
and I was in for a hundred and four
a week and a day more
I remember cause he come to see me
when they let him out
he was burnt so bad I couldn't tell
who he was till he said something
he ast if I's okay and I said Yas
we just looked at each other for a minute
then he walked off
I said Be seeing you, he just waved
three days later he drove his car
into a bridge and killed hisself
they buried him exactly one week after
they let him out and then let me out
the next day after his funeral was over

I don't have no bad scars left that show
my legs is burnt good
I still feel it I get cold
have to wear them long underwears
all year long on my legs
my hands is so thin they bleed easy
skin's about as thick as a cigarette paper
but I'm lucky I guess
all the rest is dead cept me

I went back to work for the oil
the next day because I didn't have nothing
else to do and they put me on chain
wrapping pipes, that's when I done it
I hadn't been working a hour
when this feller on the other side
thew his chain and I felt it hurt
so's I finished and took off my glove

the finger stayed in
I said You sonofabitch you done cut my finger off
I don't think he heard he didn't say nothing
well I had it I went to the man
and said That's it pay me off
oh he tried to get me to stay on
but I lost the taste
didn't care no more

it was after that I went down South
for the lectric company
got my stomach cut out and
then I come here to die
it was a pretty place, I didn't have nothing better
ever day LaVerne'd pack me a lunch
I'd draw her a map of where
I'd be if I didn't make it home
I was weak and couldn't hardly stand
so I'd drive up to the caprock edge
where I'd take off my clothes
let the sun shine on me
my muscles wouldn't heal up
on my stomach where I'd been burned
just ugly skin there you could see through
I only weight ninety six pounds
I'd lay on a quilt and look back at the valley
and just wait to be dead and have it done

you know by god I guess I'd still
be laying up there waiting
except after a while LaVerne she went
and bought these two hogs for me
she knew I'd like that
I got to coming down early to feed them
when I was up there
I'd get to thinking about the market

making money
I got so cited I come down one day early
went to looking for a boar
to get a herd started
the next day I forgot to go up and die
then pretty soon I about quit
thinking about it altogether
it just don't take much to keep
some people going

that gets us about to here
which is nearly last call
before heading home
time for one last beer
they say God takes special care
of children and idiots
I guess he's been watching out
for me and you two
by god I'll always remember them times
they was good times for the most
but I do hope to Christ
they don't never ever come back

Last Call

The two saddest words in the English language.
—from a conversation with Bill Kloefkorn

1

Tonight

moonglow
from within
softly

like a candled egg

and softly
stars diminish
until incandescence washes

the dark sky

until midnight's
lightslick
its ebb and flow

liquid

the candent universe
rolls
softly

2

Midnight
remonstrance:

there are those
I wish honestly
only to remember

being gone
and only memory

and
there are those
I wish to never remember

desiring
only their presence

lasting as long
as my life
until forever

as
I cannot imagine

living in a world
containing
only their memory

3

And you my friend
whom the gods call
into that other alone

wherever you wake
be it desert or forest
mountain or seaside

find tinder
dry moss and kindling
flint

strike a small fire which
being eternity
will flicker beyond forever

sing
your bright poem
fork your lightning dance

I will find you
sooner than later wherever
you wait in the darkness

We will sing together
delirious and off key
We will tell great lies

to shame the heavens
We will cook with wine
I promise you this

Coda

What do you honestly think
about that pile of stacked up junk?

I honestly think
it's probley one of the most beautiful things
I ever saw in my goddam life

Are you shitting me?

I shit you not

Notes

While there are dozens of allusions and references in this book to scriptural and classical authors, as well as known and recognizable writers from the middle ages through the twentieth century, certain contemporary writers are quoted and should be acknowledged.

In "The Committee to Review and Revise the Board of Education Mission Statement," the italics are from T. S. Eliot. In "Lost in Translation," the marvelous Mr. Nims is John Frederick Nims. In "From the Pickup Cab," the hero is Robert Creeley. In "Idyll," the prophet is Phillip Larkin. As far as I know and to the best of my knowledge, Jack Shit was an invention of either William Kloefkorn or my Uncle Odell Latham, who I have wanted to acknowledge as a major influence in my life for almost seventy years and am delighted to use this opportunity to fulfill that goal, even though I am sure beyond any shadow of a doubt that these words never crossed his lips.

In the poem, "The Monument to the South Plains," the images of farm implements and machinery used in the sculpture's construction are taken from poems by William Kloefkorn and by the author of this book.

Acknowledgments

The author wishes to thank the editors of the following presses and journals where the poems in this book originally appeared:

Bosque: "The Traildust Gospel"
Clover, a Literary Rag, Volume 3, Summer 2012: "At the Sign of the Flying Red Horse"
Clover, a Literary Rag, Volume 4, Winter 2012: "Monroe"
Clover, a Literary Rag, Volume 4, Summer, 2013: "Substitute Teacher".
Cutthroat: "San Antonio Incident," "Eloise Ann"
Paddlefish 2012, Number 6: "The Monument to the South Plains Series"
Paddlefish 2013, Number 7: "Driving Solo," "What They Say," "From the Pickup Cab"

"Higher Authority," "Lost in Translation," "Jacks," and "The closing Sequence: Idyll, Oil Well Fire and Last Call" originally appeared in *Narrative Magazine.*

An earlier version of "E. U. Washburn's Story: Uncle Abe" appeared in *Covenants* (with William Kloefkorn), Spoon river Poetry Press.

An earlier version of "Pain" appeared in *Day's Work*, Copper Canyon Press.

An earlier version of "The Oil Well Fire" was a part of the long-poem *Driving and Drinking*, Copper Canyon Press.

For patient, thoughtful, wonderful bordering on the magnificent readings, suggestions, encouragement, and critical reactions to this manuscript that went light years above and beyond the call of duty or friendship, copious thanks to Eleanor Wilner, a goddess incarnate; my great friends Michael Donovan and Rob Van Wagoner, who I claim as hermanos; Jon and JoDee, who have grown to be both kith and kin; the Boulder, Utah wild bunch, who tolerated my insistence on their being my first audience to hear these poems for four years; and especially Rita Jean, who stayed with me all the way both in the caressing and goading modes on this one.

About the Author

David Lee was raised in West Texas, a background he has never completely escaped, despite his varied experiences as a seminary student, a boxer and semi-pro baseball player (the only white player to ever play for the Negro League Post Texas Blue Stars) known for his knuckleball, a hog farmer, and a decorated Army veteran. Along the way he earned a Ph.D., taught at various universities, and recently retired as the Chairman of the Department of Language and Literature at Southern Utah University.

Lee was named Utah's first Poet Laureate in 1997, and has received both the Mountains & Plains Booksellers Award in Poetry and the Western States Book Award in Poetry. Lee received the Utah Governor's Award for lifetime achievement in the arts and was listed among Utah's top twelve writers of all time by the Utah Endowment for the Humanities. He is the author of twenty books of poetry. In 2004, *So Quietly the Earth* was selected for the New York Public Library's annual "Books to Remember" list. His latest, a joint collection with the late poet William Kloefkorn, is *Moments of Delicate Balance* (Wings Press, 2011).

Wings Press was founded in 1975 by Joanie Whitebird and Joseph F. Lomax, both deceased, as "an informal association of artists and cultural mythologists dedicated to the preservation of the literature of the nation of Texas." Publisher, editor and designer since 1995, Bryce Milligan is honored to carry on and expand that mission to include the finest in American writing—meaning all of the Americas, without commercial considerations clouding the choice to publish or not to publish.

Wings Press produces multicultural books, chapbooks, ebooks, CDs, and broadsides that, we hope, enlighten the human spirit and enliven the mind. Everyone ever associated with Wings has been or is a writer, and we believe that writing is a transformational art form capable of changing the world, primarily by allowing us to glimpse something of each other's souls. Good writing is innovative, insightful, open-minded and interesting. But most of all it is honest.

Likewise, Wings Press is committed to treating the planet as a partner. Thus the press uses as much recycled material as possible, from the paper on which the books are printed to the boxes in which they are shipped.

As Robert Dana wrote in *Against the Grain*, "Small press publishing is personal publishing. In essence, it's a matter of personal vision, personal taste and courage, and personal friendships." Welcome to our world.

Colophon

This first edition of *Last Call* by David Lee, has been printed on 55 pound EB natural paper containing a percentage of recycled fiber. Titles have been set in Birch type, the text in Caslon type. All Wings Press books are designed and produced by Bryce Milligan.

On-line catalogue and ordering:
www.wingspress.com

Wings Press titles are distributed
to the trade by the
Independent Publishers Group
www.ipgbook.com
and in Europe by
www.gazellebookservices.co.uk

LAST CALL

Selected Poetry by David Lee

Day's Work, 1990

Paragonah Canyon, 1990

My Town, 1995

Covenants (with William Kloefkorn), 1996

Wayburne Pig, 1997

The Fish, 1997

A Legacy of Shadow: Selected Poems, 1999

News from Down to the Café: New Poems, 1999

Incident at Thompson Slough, 2002

So Quietly the Earth, 2004

In a House Made of Time (with William Kloefkorn), 2010

Stone Wind Water, 2011

Texas Wild Flowers, 2011

Moments of Delicate Balance (with William Kloefkorn), 2011